BY JOHN MCPHEE

Annals of the Former World
Irons in the Fire
The Ransom of Russian Art
Assembling California
Looking for a Ship
The Control of Nature
Rising from the Plains
Table of Contents
La Place de la Concorde Suisse
In Suspect Terrain
Basin and Range
Giving Good Weight
Coming into the Country
The Survival of the Bark Canoe
Pieces of the Frame
The Curve of Binding Energy
The Deltoid Pumpkin Seed
Encounters with the Archdruid
The Crofter and the Laird
Levels of the Game
A Roomful of Hovings
The Pine Barrens
Oranges
The Headmaster
A Sense of Where You Are

The John McPhee Reader
The Second John McPhee Reader

A Sense of Where You Are

A
SENSE
OF WHERE
YOU ARE

A Profile of
Bill Bradley at Princeton
by
JOHN McPHEE

Farrar, Straus and Giroux
New York

Farrar, Straus and Giroux
18 West 18th Street, New York 10011

Copyright © 1965, 1978, 1999 by John McPhee
All rights reserved
Distributed in Canada by Douglas & McIntyre Ltd.
Printed in the United States of America
Published in 1978 by Farrar, Straus and Giroux
First paperback edition, 1978
This edition, 1999

The second chapter of this book originally
appeared as a Profile in The New Yorker.
The author wishes to thank the magazine
for permission to reprint it.

The Library of Congress has cataloged the hardcover edition as follows:
McPhee, John, 1931–
    A sense of where you are; a profile of William Warren Bradley,
by John McPhee.
    p. cm.
    ISBN-13: 978-0-374-26093-4
    ISBN-10: 0-374-26093-1
    1. Bradley, Bill, 1943–.

GV885 .M28
796.323630924
                                                                    65019337

Paperback ISBN-13: 978-0-374-52689-4
Paperback ISBN-10: 0-374-52689-3

www.fsgbooks.com

8   10   12   14   16   15   13   11   9

To
Harry Roemer McPhee

Contents

About This Edition

A Sense of Where You Are has been continuously in print since 1965. A second edition appeared in 1978, when addenda of photographs and caption material were included to suggest Bill Bradley's activities in the intervening years. And now this third edition, coming after two more decades, adds a photographic section that relates to Bradley's eighteen years in the United States Senate. The book's text is, and has always been, the 1965 original: a portrait of Bradley as he was in college—student and athlete. It is a story that suggests the abundant beginnings of his professional careers in sport and politics. This note is written here so that no reader coming upon the book for the first time will expect other contents.

J.A.McP.

One January in the nineteen-eighties, I was in Laramie, Wyoming, working on a project with the Rocky Mountain geologist J. David Love, whose U.S. Geological Survey office was on the campus of the University of Wyoming. One evening, the Loves invited a dozen friends over for an informal party, and among them was an oversized English professor who was dressed in state-of-the-art basketball shoes and silky sweats—all he needed, evidently, to deal with a Wyoming winter. This was John Edgar Wideman, already a well-established novelist and non-fiction writer, and ultimately the author of *Brothers & Keepers*, *Two Cities*, *Fatheralong*, *Philadelphia Fire*, and *The Homewood Trilogy*. He said he was on his way after the party to a "pick-up game" at the university. Wideman was forty-five but fit. You didn't have to be an N.B.A. scout to sense that the pick-up game would be the sort that attracts spectators.

Wideman was the University of Pennsylvania's basketball captain in 1963, when Bill Bradley was a sophomore at Princeton. Two years later, Bradley followed Wideman to Oxford University, where they were Rhodes Scholars. They got to know each other well, and played a season of basketball together for Oxford.

Now, in the geologist's living room in Laramie, Wideman told me that he had not seen Bradley since Bradley's playing days with the New York Knickerbockers, and, moreover, Wideman was not at all sure he wanted to. Bradley had gone into politics, Wideman explained, and had been a United States Senator for—at that moment—ten years. Wideman remarked that he had liked and admired Bradley so much that he frankly feared the changes he might discover: the all-too-familiar results of the mutating effects of political life.

I remember saying, "You've got nothing to worry about. Look him up some time. You'll see."

John McPhee
Princeton, N.J.
January, 1999

A Sense of Where You Are

1. *Incentive*

My father, for fourteen years or so, has served as physician to United States Olympic teams. And for more than forty years, before his retirement in June of 1964, he was a physician to college athletes, almost all of that time at Princeton. I know that he greatly admires excellence in athletes, and that he would regularly become quite caught up in the evolution of a Princeton team's season, its hopes for a championship, and the kind of performance an individual might be sustaining; but these things were discernible only in highly indirect ways. He has a taciturnity celebrated in his circle, and he can watch, say, a Princeton halfback go ninety-eight yards for a touchdown without even faintly showing on the surface the ex-

3

citement he feels within him. In fact, from the late thirties, which is as far back as I can remember, until the winter of 1962, I had never heard him actually make a direct statement of praise about any athlete, let alone make high claims, proud or otherwise, for an athlete's abilities. Then the phone rang one day in my apartment in New York, where I had been living for some years, and my father was on the other end, saying, "There's a freshman basketball player down here who is the best basketball player who has ever been near here and may be one of the best ever. You ought to come down and see him."

I remember being so surprised that I felt more worried about my father than interested in the basketball player. Finally, I said, "What's his name?"

"What difference does that make? They're playing Penn tomorrow night at six-thirty."

Freshman basketball, in my own time, a dozen years earlier, had not been a spectator sport at Princeton. A player's roommates might turn up, or his parents, if they lived nearby, but the grandstands were empty and the sound of the dribbling used to echo while the freshmen played. On the night of the game with Pennsylvania, I showed up at about six-twenty-five. There was a large crowd outside the gym and, inside, the stands were already filled. My father was holding a seat for me, and by the time I got to it the game had already begun. I sat down and purposely didn't ask which player I was supposed to watch, because that would have diminished the pleasure of discovery, and it was, in fact, something like this that my father had in mind when he had cut me off so abruptly on the phone. I watched the general flow on the court for a while, and it was soon clear enough who had drawn the crowd, and that he was the most graceful and classical basketball player who had ever been near Princeton, to say the very least. Every motion developed in its simplest form. Every motion repeated itself precisely when he used it again. He was remarkably fast, but he ran easily. His passes were so good that they were difficult to follow. Every so often, and not often enough, I thought, he stopped and went high into the air with the ball, his arms rising until his hands were at right angles to one another and high above him, and a long jump shot would go into the net. My father, once a college basketball player himself, was so moved by this that he nudged me with his elbow. It was not the two points, obviously enough—it was the form and the manner with which they had been scored. I looked from the boy's number down to the mimeographed sheet in my hand. His name was Bill Bradley. He was six feet, five inches tall. And he came from Crystal City, Missouri.

I learned later that the general manager of the St. Louis Hawks had declared Bradley to be of professional calibre when he was still in high school, and that is how Bradley always seemed at Princeton, at home on the court and under control even when his own game was cold, which it sometimes was. To me, Bradley's appeal was grounded in the fact that he was a pleasure to watch no matter what was happening on the scoreboard. My own feeling for basketball had faded almost to nothing over the years because the game seemed to me to have lost its balance, as players became taller and more powerful, and scores increased until it was rare when a professional team hit less than a hundred points, win or lose; it impressed me as a glut of scoring, with few patterns of attack and almost no defense any more. The players, in a sense, had gotten better than the game, and the game had become uninteresting. Moreover, it attracted exhibitionists who seemed to be more intent on amazing a crowd with aimless prestidigitation than with advancing their team by giving a sound performance. Basketball had once consumed about ninety-two percent of my time, and I had played on high school and prep school teams, only as a freshman in college, and later, curiously enough, on the team of Cambridge University, in England; but, despite all this obvious affection for the game, what had happened to me in later years as a spectator was not really a disillusionment so much as a death of interest. That, at any rate, is how I felt until 1962. After watching Bradley play several times, even when he was eighteen, it seemed to me that I had been watching all the possibilities of the game that I had ever imagined, and then some. His play was integral. There was nothing missing. He not only worked hard on defense, for example, he worked hard on defense when the other team was hopelessly beaten. He did all kinds of things he didn't have to do simply because those were the dimensions of the game.

I decided to write about him after the Princeton-St. Joseph's game in the national tournament in 1963, in which, at the end of his first college season, he showed how few players there had ever been like him. But that was not incentive enough. In the course of the year since I had first heard of him, I had learned that—as one of his classmates later put it—basketball was more a part of him than he a part of basketball. The most interesting thing about Bill Bradley was not just that he was a great basketball player, but that he succeeded so amply in other things that he was doing at the same time, reached a more promising level of attainment, and, in the end, put basketball aside because he had something better to do.

A year went by before I actually got started. In the early summer of 1964, he was working in Washington and he appeared in Princeton almost every weekend, beginning the research for his senior thesis. As frequently as he could, he came out to my home, which by then was no longer in New York but in the countryside near Princeton, and talked for hours on end. I told him that the eventual story would depend heavily on what he could contribute, and that I wanted to try to build a sense of the game itself around him rather than merely say how good he was at playing it, and that he would have to be an articulate teacher if the project were to succeed at all, since the difference between basketball as he understood it and basketball as I understood it was obviously large.

It took him a while to become enthusiastic, but when he did, he spent hours inventing game situations, then pacing his way through them, taking perhaps fifteen minutes to describe what would occur in a single two-second sequence, then stringing the sequences together. He was putting in two hours a day at the time in preparation for the Olympic games in the autumn, so he went on talking in the afternoons in the gyms at Princeton and at the Lawrenceville School five miles away. When I visited him in August in Crystal City, he would stay up until three and four in the morning doing reverse pivots, making back door plays with chairs as opponents, and shooting imaginary basketballs at imaginary baskets on wallpapered walls—the one situation in which all basketball players never miss a shot. His contribution, then, was everything that any writer could have hoped for. He added to it when he came home from Tokyo. Breaching an ordinarily sensible custom, I showed him the manuscript before I turned it in, because I was anxious for the technical detail to be checked over by an outstanding basketball player and he was the nearest one. He did the job quickly. He ran one finger down the middle of each page, reading, I would guess, ten or eleven pages a minute, completely ignoring all the passages about his personality and all the other things that ordinarily make it a poor idea to show an unpublished story to its subject. Picking out eight or ten technical flaws along the way, he caught all that there apparently were. Handing back the manuscript, he said he looked forward to reading it.

2. Profile

The basketball locker room in the gymnasium at Princeton has no blackboard, no water fountain, and, in fact, no lockers. Up on the main floor, things go along in the same vein. Collapsible grandstands pull out of the walls and crowd up to the edge of the court. Jolly alumni sometimes wander in just before a game begins, sit down on the players' bench, and are permitted to stay there. The players themselves are a little slow getting started each year, because if they try to do some practicing on their own during the autumn they find the gymnasium full of graduate students who know their rights and won't move over. When a fellow does get some action, it can be dangerous. The gym is so poorly designed that a scrimmaging player can be knocked down one of two flights of concrete stairs. It hardly seems possible, but at the moment this scandalous milieu includes William Warren Bradley, who is the best amateur basketball player in the United States and among the better players, amateur or professional, in the history of the sport.*

Bill Bradley is what college students nowadays call a superstar, and the thing that distinguishes him from other such paragons is not so much that he has happened into the Ivy League as that he is a superstar at all. For one thing, he has overcome the disadvantage of wealth. A great basketball player, almost by definition, is someone who has grown up in a constricted world, not for lack of vision or ambition but for lack of money; his environment has been limited to home, gym, and playground, and it has forced upon him, as a developing basketball player, the discipline of having nothing else to do. Bradley must surely be the only great basketball player who wintered regularly in Palm Beach until he was thirteen years old.

* Too late for Bradley, Princeton constructed a nine-and-a-half-million-dollar gymnasium, which contains a room so large and lofty that a football game could be played in it, punts and all.

His home is in Crystal City, Missouri, a small town on the Mississippi River about thirty miles south of St. Louis, and at Crystal City High School, despite the handicap of those earlier winters, he became one of the highest-scoring players in the records of secondary-school basketball. More than seventy colleges tried to recruit him, nearly all of them offering him scholarships. Instead, Bradley chose a school that offered him no money at all. Scholarships at Princeton are given only where there is financial need, and nearly half of Princeton's undergraduates have them, but Bradley is ineligible for one, because his father, the president of a bank, is a man of more than comfortable means.

Bradley says that when he was seventeen he came to realize that life was much longer than a few winters of basketball. He is quite serious in his application to the game, but he has wider interests and, particularly, bigger ambitions. He is a history student, interested in politics, and last July he worked for Governor Scranton in Washington. He was once elected president of the Missouri Association of Student Councils, and he is the sort of boy who, given a little more time, would have been in the forefront of undergraduate political life; as it is, he has been a considerable asset to Princeton quite apart from his feats in the gymnasium, through his work for various campus organizations. In a way that athletes in Ivy League colleges sometimes do not, he fits into the university as a whole.

Now his Princeton years are coming to an end, and lately he has been under more recruitment pressure—this time, of course, from the National Basketball Association. In September, however, on the eve of his departure for Tokyo, where, as a member of the United States basketball team, he won a gold medal in the Olympic Games, he filed an application with the American Rhodes Scholarship Committee. Just before Christmas, he was elected a Rhodes Scholar. This has absolutely nonplussed the New York Knickerbockers, who for some time had been suffering delusions of invincibility, postdated to the autumn of 1965, when, they assumed, Bradley would join their team. Two years ago, when the Syracuse Nationals wanted to transfer their franchise and become the Philadelphia '76ers, the Knicks refused to give their approval until they had received a guarantee that they would retain territorial rights to Bradley, whose college is one mile closer to Philadelphia than it is to New York. Bradley says he knows that he will very much miss not being able to play the game at its highest level, but, as things are now, if Bradley plays basketball at all next year, it will be for Oxford.

To many eastern basketball fans, what the Knickerbockers will be missing has not always been as apparent as it is today. Three seasons ago, when Bradley, as a Princeton freshman, broke a free-throw record for the sport of basketball at large, much of the outside world considered it a curious but not necessarily significant achievement. In game after game, he kept sinking foul shots without missing, until at the end of the season he had made fifty-seven straight —one more than the previous all-time high, which had been set by a member of the professional Syracuse Nationals.

The following year, as a varsity player, he averaged a little over twenty-seven points per game, and it became clear that he was the best player ever to have been seen in the Ivy League—better than Yale's Tony Lavelli, who was one of the leading scorers in

the United States in 1949, or Dartmouth's Rudy
LaRusso, who is now a professional with the Los
Angeles Lakers. But that still wasn't saying a lot.
Basketball players of the highest calibre do not gravi-
tate to the Ivy League, and excellence within its
membership has seldom been worth more, nationally,
than a polite smile. However, Ivy teams play early-
season games outside their league, and at the end of
the season the Ivy League champion competes in the
tournament of the National Collegiate Athletic Association, which brings together the outstanding teams
in the country and eventually establishes the national
champion. Gradually, during his sophomore and
junior years, Bradley's repeatedly superior performances in these games eradicated all traces of the
notion that he was merely a parochial accident and
would have been just another player if he had gone
to a big basketball school. He has scored as heavily
against non-Ivy opponents as he has against Ivy
League teams—forty points against Army, thirty-two
against Villanova, thirty-three against Davidson,
thirty against Wake Forest, thirty-one against Navy,
thirty-four against St. Louis, thirty-six against Syra-

cuse, and forty-six in a rout of the University of Texas. Last season, in the Kentucky Invitational Tournament, at the University of Kentucky, Princeton defeated Wisconsin largely because Bradley was busy scoring forty-seven points—a record for the tournament. The size of this feat can be understood if one remembers that Kentucky has won more national championships than any other university and regularly invites the best competition it can find to join in its holiday games.

An average of twenty points in basketball is comparable to baseball's criterion for outstanding pitchers, whose immortality seems to be predicated on their winning twenty games a year. Bradley scored more points last season than any other college basketball player, and his average was 32.3 per game. If Bradley's shooting this season comes near matching his accomplishment of last year, he will become one of the three highest-scoring players in the history of college basketball.

Those who have never seen him are likely to assume that he is seven and a half feet tall—the sort of elaborate weed that once all but choked off the game.

With an average like his, it would be fair to imagine him spending his forty minutes of action merely stuffing the ball into the net. But the age of the goon is over. Bradley is six feet five inches tall—the third-tallest player on the Princeton team. He is perfectly coördinated, and he is unbelievably accurate at every kind of shot in the basketball repertory. He does much of his scoring from considerable distances, and when he sends the ball toward the basket, the odds are that it is going in, since he has made more than half the shots he has attempted as a college player. With three, or even four, opponents clawing at him, he will rise in the air, hang still for a moment, and release a high parabola jump shot that almost always seems to drop into the basket with an equal margin to the rim on all sides. Against Harvard last February, his ninth long shot from the floor nicked the rim slightly on its way into the net. The first eight had gone cleanly through the center. He had missed none at all. He missed several as the evening continued, but when his coach finally took him out, he had scored fifty-one points. In a game twenty-four hours earlier, he had begun a thirty-nine point performance by hitting his first four straight. Then he missed a couple. Then he made ten consecutive shots, totally demoralizing Dartmouth.

Bradley is one of the few basketball players who have ever been appreciatively cheered by a disinterested away-from-home crowd while warming up. This curious event occurred last March, just before Princeton eliminated the Virginia Military Institute, the year's Southern Conference champion, from the N.C.A.A. championships. The game was played in Philadelphia and was the last of a tripleheader. The people there were worn out, because most of them were emotionally committed to either Villanova or Temple—two local teams that had just been involved in enervating battles with Providence and Connecticut, respectively, scrambling for a chance at the rest of the country. A group of Princeton boys shooting basketballs miscellaneously in preparation for still another game hardly promised to be a high point of the evening, but Bradley, whose routine in the warmup time is a gradual crescendo of activity, is more interesting to watch before a game than most players are in play. In Philadelphia that night, what he did was, for him, anything but unusual. As he does before all games, he began by shooting set shots close to the basket, gradually moving back until he was shooting long sets from twenty feet out, and nearly all of them dropped into the net with an almost mechanical rhythm of accuracy. Then he began a series of expandingly difficult jump shots, and one jumper after another went cleanly through the basket with so few exceptions that the crowd began to murmur. Then he started to perform whirling reverse moves before another cadence of almost steadily accurate jump shots, and the murmur increased. Then he began to sweep hook shots into the air. He moved in a semicircle around the court. First with his right hand, then with his left, he tried seven of these long, graceful shots—the most difficult ones in the orthodoxy of basketball—and ambidextrously made them all. The game had not even begun, but the presumably unimpressible Philadelphians were applauding like an audience at an opera.

Bradley has a few unorthodox shots, too. He dislikes flamboyance, and, unlike some of basketball's greatest stars, has apparently never made a move merely to attract attention. While some players are eccentric in their shooting, his shots, with only occasional exceptions, are straightforward and unexaggerated. Nonetheless, he does make something of a spectacle of himself when he moves in rapidly parallel to the baseline, glides through the air with his back to the basket, looks for a teammate he can pass to, and, finding none, tosses the ball into the basket over one shoulder, like a pinch of salt. Only when the ball is actually dropping through the net does he look around to see what has happened, on the chance that something might have gone wrong, in which case he would have to go for the rebound. That shot has the essential characteristics of a wild accident, which is what many people stubbornly think they have witnessed until they see him do it for the third time in a row. All shots in basketball are supposed to have names—the set, the hook, the lay-up, the jump shot, and so on—and one weekend last July, while Bradley was in Princeton working on his senior thesis and putting in some time in the Princeton gymnasium to keep himself in form for the Olympics, I asked him what he called his over-the-shoulder shot. He said that he had never heard a name for it, but that he had seen Oscar Robertson, of the Cincinnati Royals, and Jerry West, of the Los Angeles Lakers, do it, and had worked it out for himself. He went on to say that it is a much simpler shot than it appears to be, and, to illustrate, he tossed a ball over his shoulder and into the basket while he was talking and looking me in the eye. I retrieved the ball and handed it back to him. "When you have played basketball for a while, you don't need to look at the basket when you are in close like this," he said, throwing it over his shoulder again and right through the hoop. "You develop a sense of where you are."

Bradley is not an innovator. Actually, basketball has had only a few innovators in its history—players like Hank Luisetti, of Stanford, whose introduction in 1936 of the running one-hander did as much to open up the game for scoring as the forward pass did for football; and Joe Fulks, of the old Philadelphia Warriors, whose twisting two-handed heaves, made while he was leaping like a salmon, were the beginnings of the jump shot, which seems to be basketball's ultimate weapon. Most basketball players appropriate fragments of other players' styles, and thus develop their own. This is what Bradley has done, but one of the things that set him apart from nearly everyone else is that the process has been conscious rather than osmotic. His jump shot, for example, has had two principal influences. One is Jerry West, who has one of the best jumpers in basketball. At a summer basketball camp in Missouri some years ago, West told Bradley that he always gives an extra hard bounce to the last dribble before a jump shot, since this seems to catapult him to added height. Bradley has been doing that ever since. Terry Dischinger, of the Detroit Pistons, has told Bradley that he always slams his foot to the floor on the last step before a jump shot, because this stops his momentum and thus prevents drift. Drifting while aloft is the mark of a sloppy jump shot.

Bradley's graceful hook shot is a masterpiece of eclecticism. It consists of the high-lifted knee of the Los Angeles Lakers' Darrall Imhoff, the arms of Bill Russell, of the Boston Celtics, who extends his idle hand far under his shooting arm and thus magically stabilizes the shot, and the general corporeal form of

Kentucky's Cotton Nash, a rookie this year with the Lakers. Bradley carries his analyses of shots further than merely identifying them with pieces of other people. "There are five parts to the hook shot," he explains to anyone who asks. As he continues, he picks up a ball and stands about eighteen feet from a basket. "Crouch," he says, crouching, and goes on to demonstrate the other moves. "Turn your head to look for the basket, step, kick, follow through with your arms." Once, as he was explaining this to me, the ball curled around the rim and failed to go in.

"What happened then?" I asked him.

"I didn't kick high enough," he said.

"Do you always know exactly why you've missed a shot?"

"Yes," he said, missing another one.

"What happened that time?"

"I was talking to you. I didn't concentrate. The secret of shooting is concentration."

His set shot is borrowed from Ed Macauley, who was a St. Louis University All-American in the late forties and was later a star member of the Boston Celtics and the St. Louis Hawks. Macauley runs the basketball camp Bradley first went to when he was fifteen. In describing the set shot, Bradley is probably quoting a Macauley lecture. "Crouch like Groucho Marx," he says. "Go off your feet a few inches. You shoot with your legs. Your arms merely guide the ball." Bradley says that he has more confidence in his set shot than in any other. However, he seldom uses it, because he seldom has to. A set shot is a long shot, usually a twenty-footer, and Bradley, with his speed and footwork, can almost always take some other kind of shot, closer to the basket. He will take set shots when they are given to him, though. Two seasons ago, Davidson lost to Princeton, using a compact zone defense that ignored the remoter areas of the court. In one brief sequence, Bradley sent up seven set shots, missing only one. The missed one happened to rebound in Bradley's direction, and he leaped up, caught it with one hand, and scored.

Even his lay-up shot has an ancestral form; he is full of admiration for "the way Cliff Hagan pops up anywhere within six feet of the basket," and he tries to do the same. Hagan is a former Kentucky star who now plays for the St. Louis Hawks. Because opposing teams always do everything they can to stop Bradley, he gets an unusual number of foul shots. When he was in high school, he used to imitate Bob Pettit, of the St. Louis Hawks, and Bill Sharman of the Boston Celtics, but now his free throw is more or less his own. With his left foot back about eighteen inches— "wherever it feels comfortable," he says—he shoots with a deep-bending rhythm of knees and arms, one-handed, his left hand acting as a kind of gantry for the ball until the moment of release. What is most interesting, though, is that he concentrates his attention on one of the tiny steel eyelets that are welded under the rim of the basket to hold the net to the hoop—on the center eyelet, of course—before he lets fly. One night, he scored over twenty points on free throws alone; Cornell hacked at him so heavily that he was given twenty-one free throws, and he made all twenty-one, finishing the game with a total of thirty-seven points.

When Bradley, working out alone, practices his set shots, hook shots, and jump shots, he moves systematically from one place to another around the basket, his distance from it being appropriate to the shot, and he does not permit himself to move on until he has made at least ten shots out of thirteen from each location. He applies this standard to every kind of shot, with either hand, from any distance. Many basketball players, including reasonably good ones, could spend five years in a gym and not make ten out of thirteen left-handed hook shots, but that is part of Bradley's daily routine. He talks to himself while he is shooting, usually reminding himself to concentrate but sometimes talking to himself the way every high-school j.v. basketball player has done since the dim twenties—more or less imitating a radio announcer, and saying, as he gathers himself up for a shot, "It's pandemonium in Dillon Gymnasium. The clock is running out. He's up with a jumper. Swish!"

Last summer, the floor of the Princeton gym was being resurfaced, so Bradley had to put in several practice sessions at the Lawrenceville School. His first afternoon at Lawrenceville, he began by shooting fourteen-foot jump shots from the right side. He got off to a bad start, and he kept missing them. Six in a row hit the back rim of the basket and bounced out. He stopped, looking discomfited, and seemed to be making an adjustment in his mind. Then he went up for another jump shot from the same spot and hit it cleanly. Four more shots went in without a miss, and then he paused and said, "You want to know something? That basket is about an inch and a half low." Some weeks later, I went back to Lawrenceville with a steel tape, borrowed a stepladder, and measured the height of the basket. It was nine feet ten and seven-eighths inches above the floor, or one and one-eighth inches too low.

Being a deadly shot with either hand and knowing how to make the moves and fakes that clear away the defense are the primary skills of a basketball player, and any player who can do these things half as well as Bradley can has all the equipment he needs to make a college team. Many high-scoring basketball players, being able to make so obvious and glamorous a contribution to their team in the form of point totals, don't bother to develop the other skills of the game, and leave subordinate matters like defense and playmaking largely to their teammates. Hence, it is usually quite easy to parse a basketball team. Bringing the ball up the floor are playmaking backcourt men—selfless fellows who can usually dribble so adeptly that they can just about freeze the ball by themselves, and who can also throw passes through the eye of a needle and can always be counted on to feed the ball to a star at the right moment. A star is often a point-hungry gunner, whose first instinct when he gets the ball is to fire away, and whose playing creed might be condensed to "When in doubt, shoot." Another, with legs like automobile springs, is part of the group because of an unusual ability to go high for rebounds. Still another may not be especially brilliant on offense but has defensive equipment that could not be better if he were carrying a trident and a net.

The point-hungry gunner aside, Bradley is all these. He is a truly complete basketball player. He can play in any terrain; in the heavy infighting near the basket, he is master of all the gestures of the big men, and toward the edge of play he shows that he has all the fast-moving skills of the little men, too. With remarkable speed for six feet five, he can steal the ball and break into the clear with it on his own;

as a dribbler, he can control the ball better with his left hand than most players can with their right; he can go down court in the middle of a fast break and fire passes to left and right, closing in on the basket, the timing of his passes too quick for the spectator's eye. He plays any position—up front, in the post, in the backcourt. And his playmaking is a basic characteristic of his style. His high-scoring totals are the result of his high percentage of accuracy, not of an impulse to shoot every time he gets the ball.

He passes as generously and as deftly as any player in the game. When he is dribbling, he can pass accurately without first catching the ball. He can also manage almost any pass without appearing to cock his arm, or even bring his hand back. He just seems to flick his fingers and the ball is gone. Other Princeton players aren't always quite expecting Bradley's passes when they arrive, for Bradley is usually thinking a little bit ahead of everyone else on the floor. When he was a freshman, he was forever hitting his teammates on the mouth, the temple, or the back of the head with passes as accurate as they were surprising. His teammates have since sharpened their own faculties, and these accidents seldom happen now. "It's rewarding to play with him," one of them says. "If you get open, you'll get the ball." And, with all the defenders in between, it sometimes seems as if the ball has passed like a ray through several walls.

Bradley's play has just one somewhat unsound aspect, and it is the result of his mania for throwing the ball to his teammates. He can't seem to resist throwing a certain number of passes that are based on nothing but theory and hope; in fact, they are referred to by the Princeton coaching staff as Bradley's hope passes. They happen, usually, when something has gone just a bit wrong. Bradley is recovering a loose ball, say, with his back turned to the other Princeton players. Before he turned it, he happened to notice a screen, or pick-off, being set by two of his teammates, its purpose being to cause one defensive man to collide with another player and thus free an offensive man to receive a pass and score. Computations whir in Bradley's head. He hasn't time to look, but the screen, as he saw it developing, seemed to be working, so a Princeton man should now be in the clear, running toward the basket with one arm up.

He whips the ball over his shoulder to the spot where the man ought to be. Sometimes a hope pass goes flying into the crowd, but most of the time they hit the receiver right in the hand, and a gasp comes from several thousand people. Bradley is sensitive about such dazzling passes, because they look flashy, and an edge comes into his voice as he defends them. "When I was halfway down the court, I saw a man out of the corner of my eye who had on the same color shirt I did," he said recently, explaining how he happened to fire a scoring pass while he was falling out of bounds. "A little later, when I threw the pass, I threw it to the spot where that man should have been if he had kept going and done his job. He was there. Two points."

Since it appears that by nature Bradley is a passer first and a scorer second, he would probably have scored less at a school where he was surrounded by other outstanding players. When he went to Princeton, many coaches mourned his loss not just to themselves but to basketball, but as things have worked out, much of his national prominence has been precipitated by his playing for Princeton, where he has had to come through with points in order to keep his team from losing. He starts slowly, as a rule. During much of the game, if he has a clear shot, fourteen feet from the basket, say, and he sees a teammate with an equally clear shot ten feet from the basket, he sends the ball to the teammate. Bradley apparently does not stop to consider that even though the other fellow is closer to the basket he may be far more likely to miss the shot. This habit exasperates his coaches until they clutch their heads in despair. But Bradley is doing what few people ever have done—he is playing basketball according to the foundation pattern of the game. Therefore, the shot goes to the closer man. Nothing on earth can make him change until Princeton starts to lose. Then he will concentrate a little more on the basket.

Something like this happened in Tokyo last October, when the United States Olympic basketball team came close to being beaten by Yugoslavia. The Yugoslavian team was reasonably good—better than the Soviet team, which lost to the United States in the final—and it heated up during the second half. With two minutes to go, Yugoslavia cut the United States' lead to two points. Bradley was on the bench at the time, and Henry Iba, the Oklahoma State coach, who was coach of the Olympic team, sent him in. During much of the game, he had been threading passes to others, but at that point, he says, he felt that he had to try to do something about the score. Bang, bang, bang—he hit a running one-hander, a seventeen-foot jumper, and a lay-up on a fast break, and the United States won by eight points.

Actually, the United States basketball squad encountered no real competition at the Olympics, despite all sorts of rumbling cumulus beforehand to the effect that some of the other teams, notably Russia's, were made up of men who had been playing together for years and were now possibly good enough to defeat an American Olympic basketball team for the first time. But if the teams that the Americans faced were weaker than advertised, there were nonetheless individual performers of good calibre, and it is a further index to Bradley's completeness as a basketball player that Henry Iba, a defensive specialist as a coach, regularly assigned him to guard the stars of the other nations. "He didn't show too much tact at defense when he started, but he's a coach's basketball player, and he came along," Iba said after he had returned to Oklahoma. "And I gave him the toughest man in every game."

Yugoslavia's best man was a big forward who liked to play in the low post, under the basket. Bradley went into the middle with him, crashing shoulders under the basket, and held him to thirteen points while scoring eighteen himself. Russia's best man was Yuri Korneyev, whose specialty was driving; that is, he liked to get the ball somewhere out on the edge of the action and start for the basket with it like a fullback, blasting everything out of the way until he got close enough to ram in a point-blank shot. With six feet five inches and two hundred and forty pounds to drive, Korneyev was what Iba called "a real good driver." Bradley had lost ten pounds because of all the Olympics excitement, and Korneyev outweighed him by forty-five pounds. Korneyev kicked, pushed, shoved, bit, and scratched Bradley. "He was tough to stop," Bradley says. "After all, he was playing for his life." Korneyev got eight points.

Bradley was one of three players who had been

picked unanimously for the twelve-man Olympic team. He was the youngest member of the squad and the only undergraduate. Since his trip to Tokyo kept him away from Princeton for the first six weeks of the fall term, he had to spend part of his time reading, and the course he worked on most was Russian History 323. Perhaps because of the perspective this gave him, his attitude toward the Russian basketball team was not what he had expected it to be. With the help of three Australian players who spoke Russian, Bradley got to know several members of the Russian team fairly well, and soon he was feeling terribly sorry for them. They had a leaden attitude almost from the beginning. "All we do is play basketball," one of them told him forlornly. "After we go home, we play in the Soviet championships. Then we play in the Satellite championships. Then we play in the European championships. I would give anything for five days off." Bradley says that the Russian players also told him they were paid eighty-five dollars a month, plus housing. Given the depressed approach of the Russians, Bradley recalls, it was hard to get excited before the Russian-American final. "It

was tough to get chills," he says. "I had to imagine
we were about to play Yale." The Russians lost,
73–59.

When Bradley talks about basketball, he speaks
with authority, explaining himself much as a man of
fifty might do in discussing a profession or business.
When he talks about other things, he shows himself
to be a polite, diffident, hopeful, well-brought-up, extremely amiable, and sometimes naïve but generally
discerning young man just emerging from adoles-
cence. He was twenty-one last summer, and he seems
neither older nor younger than his age. He is pain-
fully aware of his celebrity. The nature of it and
the responsibility that it imposes are constantly
on his mind. He remembers people's names, and
greets them by name when he sees them again.
He seems to want to prove that he finds other
people interesting. "The main thing I have to pre-
vent myself from becoming is disillusioned with
transitory success," he said recently. "It's dangerous.
It's like a heavy rainstorm. It can do damage or it
can do good, permitting something to grow." He

claims that the most important thing basketball gives him at Princeton is "a real period of relief from the academic load." Because he is the sort of student who does all his academic course work, he doesn't get much sleep; in fact, he has a perilous contempt for sleep, partly because he has been told that professional basketball players get along on almost none of it. He stays up until his work is done, for if he were to retire any earlier he would be betraying the discipline he has placed upon himself. When he has had to, he has set up schedules of study that have kept him reading from 6 A.M. to midnight every day for as long as eight weeks. On his senior thesis, which is due in April (and is about Harry Truman's senatorial campaign in 1940), he has already completed more research than many students will do altogether. One of his most enviable gifts is his ability to regiment his conscious mind. After a game, for example, most college players, if they try to study, see all the action over again between the lines in their books. Bradley can, and often does, go straight to the library and work for hours, postponing his mental re-play as long as he cares to. If he feels that it's necessary, he will stay up all night before a basketball game; he did that last winter when he was completing a junior paper, and Princeton barely managed to beat a fairly unspectacular Lafayette team, because Bradley seemed almost unable to lift his arms. Princeton was losing until Bradley, finally growing wakeful, scored eight points in the last two minutes.

Ivy League basketball teams play on Friday and Saturday nights, in order to avoid travelling during the week, yet on Sunday mornings Bradley gets up and teaches a nine-thirty Sunday-school class at the First Presbyterian Church. During his sophomore and junior years at the university, he met a class of seventh-grade boys every Sunday morning that he was resident in Princeton. If the basketball bus returned to Princeton at 4:30 A.M., as it sometimes did, he would still be at the church by nine-thirty. This year, having missed two months while he was in the Far East, he is working as a spot teacher whenever he is needed. Religion, he feels, is the main source of his strength, and because he realizes that not everybody shares that feeling today, he sometimes refers to "the challenge of being in the minority in the world." He belongs to the Fellowship of Christian Athletes, an organization that was set up eight years ago, by people like Otto Graham, Bob Pettit, Branch Rickey, Bob Feller, Wilma Rudolph, Doak Walker, Rafer Johnson, and Robin Roberts, for the advancement of youth by a mixture of moral and athletic guidance. Bradley has flown all over the United States to speak to F.C.A. groups. One of his topics is a theory of his that conformists and nonconformists both lack moral courage, and another is that "the only way to solve a problem is to go through it rather than around it"—which has struck some listeners as an odd view for a basketball player to have. Nevertheless, Bradley often tells his audiences, "Basketball discipline carries over into your life," continuing, "You've got to face that you're going to lose. Losses are part of every season, and part of life. The question is, can you adjust? It is important that you don't get caught up in your own little defeats." If he seems ministerial, that is because he is. He has a firm sense of what is right, and apparently feels that he has a mission to help others see things as clearly as he does. "I don't try to be overbearing in what I believe, but, given a

chance, I will express my beliefs," he says. After the
Olympics were over, he stayed in the Far East an
extra week to make a series of speeches at universities
in Taiwan and Hong Kong.

As a news story once said of Bradley—quite accurately, it seems—he is everything his parents think he
is. He approximates what some undergraduates call a
straight arrow—a semi-pejorative term for unfortu-
nates who have no talent for vice. Nevertheless, considerable numbers of Princeton undergraduates have
told me that Bradley is easily the most widely admired student on the campus and probably the best
liked, and that his skill at basketball is not the only
way in which he atones for his moral altitude. He has
worked for the Campus Fund Drive, which is a sort
of Collegiate Gothic community chest, and for the
Orange Key Society, an organization that, among
other things, helps freshmen settle down into college
life. One effect that Bradley has had on Princeton
has been to widen noticeably the undergraduate
body's tolerance for people with high ethical standards. "He is a source of inspiration to anyone who
comes in contact with him," one of his classmates

says. "You look at yourself and you decide to do better."

Bradley has built his life by setting up and going after a series of goals, athletic and academic, which at the moment have culminated in his position on the Olympic basketball team and his Rhodes Scholarship. Of the future beyond Oxford, he says only that he wants to go to law school and later "set a Christian example by implementing my feelings within the structure of the society," adding, "I value my ultimate goals more than playing basketball." I have asked all sorts of people who know Bradley, or know about him, what they think he will be doing when he is forty. A really startling number of them, including teachers, coaches, college boys, and even journalists, give the same answer: "He will be the governor of Missouri." The chief dissent comes from people who look beyond the stepping stone of the Missouri State House and calmly tell you that Bradley is going to be President. Last spring, Leonard Shecter, of the New York *Post*, began a column by saying, "In twenty-five years or so our presidents are going to have to be better than ever. It's nice to know that Bill Bradley will be available." Edward Rapp, Bradley's high-school principal, once said, "With the help of his friends, Bill could very well be President of the United States. And without the help of his friends he might make it anyway."

Some of Bradley's classmates, who think he is a slave to his ideals, call him The Martyr, though he is more frequently addressed as Brads, Spin, Star, or Horse. He is also called Hayseed, and teased about his Missouri accent. Additional abuse is piled on him by his five roommates, who kid him by saying that his good grades are really undeserved gifts from a hero-worshipping faculty, and who insistently ask him to tell them how many points he scored in various by-gone games, implying that he knows exactly but is feigning modesty when he claims he doesn't.

He is a good-looking, dark-haired boy whose hab-its of dress give him protective coloration on the Princeton campus; like nearly everyone else, he wears khaki trousers and a white shirt. His room is always littered, and he doesn't seem to care when he runs out of things; he has been known to sleep without sheets for as long as five weeks, stretched out on a bare mattress under a hairy bit of blanket. He drives automobiles wildly. When he wastes time, he wastes it hurriedly rather than at leisure. He dates with modest frequency—girls from Smith, Wellesley, Vassar, Randolph-Macon, Manhattanville. Just before leaving his room to go dress for a basketball game, he invariably turns on his hi-fi and listens to "Climb Every Mountain," from "The Sound of Music." He is introspective, and sometimes takes himself very seriously; it is hard, too, for him to let himself go. His reserve with people he doesn't know well has often caused him to be quite inaccurately described as shy and sombre. He has an ambiguous, bemused manner that makes people wonder on occasion whether he is in earnest or just kidding; they eventually decide, as a rule, that half the time he is just kidding.

Bradley calls practically all men "Mister" whose age exceeds his own by more than a couple of years. This includes any N.B.A. players he happens to meet, Princeton trainers, and Mr. Willem Hendrik van Breda Kolff, his coach. Van Breda Kolff was a Princeton basketball star himself, some twenty years

ago, and went on to play for the New York Knickerbockers. Before returning to Princeton in 1962, he
coached at Lafayette and Hofstra. His teams at the
three colleges have won two hundred and fifty-one
games and lost ninety-six. Naturally, it was a virtually unparalleled stroke of good fortune for van
Breda Kolff to walk into his current coaching job in
the very year that Bradley became eligible to play
for the varsity team, but if the coach was lucky to have
the player, the player was also lucky to have the
coach. Van Breda Kolff, a cheerful and uncomplicated man, has a sportsman's appreciation of the
nuances of the game, and appears to feel that mere
winning is far less important than winning with
style. He is an Abstract Expressionist of basketball.
Other coaches have difficulty scouting his teams, because he does not believe in a set offense. He likes his
offense free-form.

Van Breda Kolff simply tells his boys to spread out
and keep the ball moving. "Just go fast, stay out of
one another's way, pass, move, come off guys, look
for one-on-ones, two-on-ones, two-on-twos, three-on-
threes. That's about the extent," he says. That is, in

fact, about the substance of basketball, which is almost never played as a five-man game anymore but is, rather, a constant search, conducted semi-independently by five players, for smaller combinations that will produce a score. One-on-one is the basic situation of the game—one man, with the ball, trying to score against one defensive player, who is trying to stop him, with nobody else involved. Van Breda Kolff does not think that Bradley is a great one-on-one player. "A one-on-one player is a hungry player," he explains. "Bill is not hungry. At least ninety per cent of the time, when he gets the ball, he is looking for a pass." Van Breda Kolff has often tried to force Bradley into being more of a one-on-one player, through gentle persuasion in practice, through restrained pleas during timeouts, and even through open clamor. During one game last year, when Princeton was losing and Bradley was still flicking passes, van Breda Kolff stood up and shouted, *"Will . . . you . . . shoot . . . that . . . ball?"* Bradley, obeying at once, drew his man into the vortex of a reverse pivot, and left him standing six feet behind as he made a soft, short jumper from about ten feet out.

If Bradley were more interested in his own statistics, he could score sixty or seventy-five points, or maybe even a hundred, in some of his games. But this would merely be personal aggrandizement, done at the expense of the relative balance of his own team and causing unnecessary embarrassment to the opposition, for it would only happen against an opponent that was heavily outmatched anyway. Bradley's highest point totals are almost always made when the other team is strong and the situation demands his scoring ability. He has, in fact, all the mechanical faculties a great one-on-one player needs. As van Breda Kolff will point out, for example, Bradley has "a great reverse pivot," and this is an essential characteristic of a one-on-one specialist. A way of getting rid of a defensive man who is playing close, it is a spin of the body, vaguely similar to what a football halfback does when he spins away from a would-be tackler, and almost exactly what a lacrosse player does when he "turns his man." Say that Bradley is dribbling hard toward the basket and the defensive man is all over him. Bradley turns, in order to put his body between his opponent and the ball; he con-

tinues his dribbling but shifts the ball from one hand
to the other; if his man is still crowding in on him, he
keeps on turning until he has made one full revolution and is once more headed toward the basket. This
is a reverse pivot. Bradley can execute one in less
than a second. The odds are that when he has completed the spin the defensive player will be behind
him, for it is the nature of basketball that the odds
favor the man with the ball—if he knows how to play
them.

Bradley doesn't need to complete the full revolution every time. If his man steps away from him in
anticipation of a reverse pivot, Bradley can stop dead
and make a jump shot. If the man stays close to him
but not close enough to be turned, Bradley can send
up a hook shot. If the man moves over so that he will
be directly in Bradley's path when Bradley comes out
of the turn, Bradley can scrap the reverse pivot before
he begins it, merely suggesting it with his shoulders
and then continuing his original dribble to the basket, making his man look like a pedestrian who has
leaped to get out of the way of a speeding car.

The metaphor of basketball is to be found in these

compounding alternatives. Every time a basketball player takes a step, an entire new geometry of action is created around him. In ten seconds, with or without the ball, a good player may see perhaps a hundred alternatives and, from them, make half a dozen choices as he goes along. A great player will see even more alternatives and will make more choices, and this multiradial way of looking at things can carry over into his life. At least, it carries over into Bradley's life. The very word "alternatives" bobs in and out of his speech with noticeable frequency. Before his Rhodes Scholarship came along and eased things, he appeared to be worrying about dozens of alternatives for next year. And he still fills his days with alternatives. He apparently always needs to have eight ways to jump, not because he is excessively prudent but because that is what makes the game interesting.

The reverse pivot, of course, is just one of numerous one-on-one moves that produce a complexity of possibilities. A rocker step, for example, in which a player puts one foot forward and rocks his shoulders forward and backward, can yield a set shot if the defensive man steps back, a successful drive to the basket if the defensive man comes in too close, a jump shot if he tries to compromise. A simple crossover—shifting a dribble from one hand to the other and changing direction—can force the defensive man to overcommit himself, as anyone knows who has ever watched Oscar Robertson use it to break free and score. Van Breda Kolff says that Bradley is "a great mover," and points out that the basis of all these maneuvers is footwork. Bradley has spent hundreds of hours merely rehearsing the choreography of the game—shifting his feet in the same patterns again and again, until they have worn into his motor subconscious. "The average basketball player only likes to play basketball," van Breda Kolff says. "When he's left to himself, all he wants to do is get a two-on-two or a three-on-three going. Bradley practices techniques, making himself learn and improve instead of merely having fun."

Because of Bradley's super-serious approach to basketball, his relationship to van Breda Kolff is in some respects a reversal of the usual relationship between a player and a coach. Writing to van Breda Kolff from Tokyo in his capacity as captain-elect, Bradley advised his coach that they should prepare themselves for "the stern challenge ahead." Van Breda Kolff doesn't vibrate to that sort of tune. "Basketball is a game," he says. "It is not an ordeal. I think Bradley's happiest whenever he can deny himself pleasure." Van Breda Kolff's handling of Bradley has been, in a way, a remarkable feat of coaching. One man cannot beat five men—at least not consistently—and Princeton loses basketball games. Until this season, moreover, the other material that van Breda Kolff has had at his disposal has been for the most part below even the usual Princeton standard, so the fact that his teams have won two consecutive championships is about as much to his credit as to his star's.

Van Breda Kolff says, "I try to play it just as if he were a normal player. I don't want to overlook him, but I don't want to over-look for him, either, if you see what I'm trying to say." Bradley's teammates sometimes depend on him too much, the coach explains, or, in a kind of psychological upheaval, get self-conscious about being on the court with a super-star and, perhaps to prove their independence, bring the ball up the court five or six times without passing it to him. When this happens, van Breda Kolff calls time out. "Hey, boys," he says. "What have we got an All-American for?" He refers to Bradley's stardom only when he has to, however. In the main, he takes Bradley with a calculated grain of salt. He is interested in Bradley's relative weaknesses rather than in his storied feats, and has helped him gain poise on the court, learn patience, improve his rebounding, and be more aggressive. He refuses on principle to say that Bradley is the best basketball player he has ever coached, and he is also careful not to echo the general feeling that Bradley is the most exemplary youth since Lochinvar, but he will go out of his way to tell about the reaction of referees to Bradley. "The refs watch Bradley like a hawk, but, because he never complains, they feel terrible if they make an error against him," he says. "They just love him because he is such a gentleman. They get upset if they call a bad one on him." I asked van Breda Kolff what he thought Bradley would be doing when he was forty. "I don't know," he said. "I guess he'll be the governor of Missouri."

Many coaches, on the reasonable supposition that Bradley cannot beat their teams alone, concentrate on choking off the four other Princeton players, but Bradley is good enough to rise to such occasions, as he did when he scored forty-six against Texas, making every known shot, including an eighteen-foot running hook. Some coaches, trying a standard method of restricting a star, set up four of their players in either a box-shaped or a diamond-shaped zone defensive formation and put their fifth player on Bradley, man-to-man. Wherever Bradley goes under these circumstances, he has at least two men guarding him, the man-to-man player and the fellow whose zone he happens to be passing through. This is a dangerous defense, however, because it concedes an imbalance of forces, and also because Bradley is so experienced at being guarded by two men at once that he can generally fake them both out with a single move; also, such overguarding often provides Bradley with enough free throws to give his team the margin of victory.

Most coaches have played Princeton straight, assigning their best defensive man to Bradley and letting it go at that. This is what St. Joseph's College did in the opening round of the N.C.A.A. Tournament in 1963. St. Joseph's had a strong, well-balanced team, which had lost only four games of a twenty-five-game schedule and was heavily favored to rout Princeton. The St. Joseph's player who was to guard Bradley promised his teammates that he would hold Bradley below twenty points. Bradley made twenty points in the first half.

He made another twenty points in the first sixteen minutes of the second half. In the group battles for rebounds, he won time after time. He made nearly sixty per cent of his shots, and he made sixteen out of sixteen from the foul line. The experienced St. Joseph's man could not handle him, and the whole team began to go after him in frenzied clusters. He would dribble through them, disappearing in the ruck and emerging a moment later, still dribbling, to float up toward the basket and score. If St. Joseph's forced him over toward the sideline, he would crouch, turn his head to look for the distant basket, step, kick his leg, and follow through with his arms, sending a long, high hook shot—all five parts intact—into the net. When he went up for a jump shot, St. Joseph's players would knock him off balance, but he would make the shot anyway, crash to the floor, get up, and sink the dividend foul shot, scoring three points instead of two on the play.

On defense, he guarded St. Joseph's highest-scoring player, Tom Wynne, and held him to nine points. The defense was expensive, though. An aggressive defensive player has to take the risk of committing five personal fouls, after which a player is obliged by the rules to leave the game. With just under four minutes to go, and Princeton comfortably ahead by five points, Bradley committed his fifth foul and left the court. For several minutes, the game was interrupted as the crowd stood and applauded him; the game was being played in Philadelphia, where hostility toward Princeton is ordinarily great but where the people know a folk hero when they see one. After the cheering ended, the blood drained slowly out of Princeton, whose other players could not hold the lead. Princeton lost by one point. Dr. Jack Ramsay, the St. Joseph's coach, says that Bradley's effort that night was the best game of basketball he has ever seen a college boy play.

Some people, hearing all the stories of Bradley's

great moments, go to see him play and are disappointed when he does not do something memorable at least once a minute. Actually, basketball is a hunting game. It lasts for forty minutes, and there are ten men on the court, so the likelihood is that any one player, even a superstar, will actually have the ball in his hands for only four of those minutes, or perhaps a little more. The rest of the time, a player on offense either is standing around recovering his breath or is on the move, foxlike, looking for openings, sizing up chances, attempting to screen off a defensive man— by "coming off guys," as van Breda Kolff puts it— and thus upset the balance of power.

The depth of Bradley's game is most discernible when he doesn't have the ball. He goes in and swims around in the vicinity of the basket, back and forth, moving for motion's sake, making plans and abandoning them, and always watching the distant movement of the ball out of the corner of his eye. He stops and studies his man, who is full of alertness because of the sudden break in the rhythm. The man is trying to watch both Bradley and the ball. Bradley watches the man's head. If it turns too much to the right, he moves quickly to the left. If it turns too much to the left, he goes to the right. If, ignoring the ball, the man focusses his full attention on Bradley, Bradley stands still and looks at the floor. A high-lobbed pass floats in, and just before it arrives Bradley jumps high, takes the ball, turns, and scores.

If Princeton has an out-of-bounds play under the basket, Bradley takes a position just inside the baseline, almost touching the teammate who is going to throw the ball into play. The defensive man crowds in to try to stop whatever Bradley is planning. Bradley whirls around the defensive man, blocking him out with one leg, and takes a bounce pass and lays up the score. This works only against naïve opposition, but when it does work it is a marvel to watch.

To receive a pass from a backcourt man, Bradley moves away from the basket and toward one side of the court. He gets the ball, gives it up, goes into the center, and hovers there awhile. Nothing happens. He goes back to the corner. He starts toward the backcourt again to receive a pass like the first one. His man, who is eager and has been through this before, moves out toward the backcourt a step ahead of Bradley. This is a defensive error. Bradley isn't going that way; he was only faking. He heads straight for the basket, takes a bounce pass, and scores. This maneuver is known in basketball as going back door. Bradley is able to go back door successfully and often, because of his practiced footwork. Many players, once their man has made himself vulnerable, rely on surprise alone to complete a backdoor play, and that isn't always enough. Bradley's fake looks for all the world like the beginning of a trip to the outside; then, when he goes for the basket, he has all the freedom he needs. When he gets the ball after breaking free, other defensive players naturally leave their own men and try to stop him. In these three-on-two or two-on-one situations, the obvious move is to pass to a teammate who has moved into a position to score. Sometimes, however, no teammate has moved, and Bradley sees neither a pass nor a shot, so he veers around and goes back and picks up his own man. "I take him on into the corner for a one-on-one," he says, imagining what he might do. "I move toward the free-throw line on a dribble. If the man is overplaying me to my right, I reverse pivot and go in for a left-handed lay-up.

If the man is playing even with me, but off me a few feet, I take a jump shot. If the man is playing me good defense—honest—and he's on me tight, I keep going. I give him a head-and-shoulder fake, keep going all the time, and drive to the basket, or I give him a head-and-shoulder fake and take a jump shot. Those are all the things you need—the fundamentals."

Bradley develops a relationship with his man that is something like the relationship between a yoyoist and his yoyo. "I'm on the side of the floor," he postulates, "and I want to play with my man a little bit, always knowing where the ball is but not immediately concerned with getting it. Basketball is a game of two or three men, and you have to know how to stay out of a play and not clutter it up. I cut to the baseline. My man will follow me. I'll cut up to the high-post position. He'll follow me. I'll cut to the low-post position. He'll follow me. I'll go back out to my side position. He'll follow. I'll fake to the center of the floor and go hard to the baseline, running my man into a pick set at the low-post position. I'm not running him into a pick in order to get free for a shot —I'm doing it simply to irritate him. I come up on the other side of the basket, looking to see if a teammate feels that I'm open. They can't get the ball to me at that instant. Now my man is back with me. I go out to the side. I set a screen for the guard. He sees the situation. He comes toward me. He dribbles hard past me, running his man into my back. I feel the contact. My man switches off me, leaving the pass lane open for a split second. I go hard to the basket and take a bounce pass for a shot. Two points."

Because Bradley's inclination to analyze every gesture in basketball is fairly uncommon, other players look at him as if they think him a little odd when he seeks them out after a game and asks them to show him what they did in making a move that he particularly admired. They tell him that they're not sure what he is talking about, and that even if they could remember, they couldn't possibly explain, so the best offer they can make is to go back to the court, try to set up the situation again, and see what it was that provoked his appreciation. Bradley told me about this almost apologetically, explaining that he had no choice but to be analytical in order to be in the game at all. "I don't have that much natural ability," he

said, and went on to tell a doleful tale about how his
legs lacked spring, how he was judged among the
worst of the Olympic candidates in ability to get high
off the floor, and so on, until he had nearly convinced
me that he was a motor moron. In actuality, Bradley
does have certain natural advantages. He has been six
feet five since he was fifteen years old, so he had most
of his high-school years in which to develop his co-
ördination, and it is now exceptional for a tall man.
His hand span, measuring only nine and a half
inches, does not give him the wraparound control that
basketball players like to have, but, despite relatively
unimpressive shoulders and biceps, he is unusually
strong, and he can successfully mix with almost anyone in the Greco-Roman battles under the back-
boards.

His most remarkable natural gift, however, is his
vision. During a game, Bradley's eyes are always a
glaze of panoptic attention, for a basketball player
needs to look at everything, focussing on nothing,
until the last moment of commitment. Beyond this,
it is obviously helpful to a basketball player to be able
to see a little more than the next man, and the remark

is frequently made about basketball superstars that they have unusual peripheral vision. People used to say that Bob Cousy, the immortal backcourt man of the Boston Celtics, could look due east and enjoy a sunset. Ed Macauley once took a long auto trip with Cousy when they were teammates, and in the course of it Cousy happened to go to sleep sitting up. Macauley swears that Cousy's eyelids, lowered as far as they would go, failed to cover his coleopteran eyes.

Bradley's eyes close normally enough, but his astounding passes to teammates have given him, too, a reputation for being able to see out of the back of his head. To discover whether there was anything to all the claims for basketball players' peripheral vision, I asked Bradley to go with me to the office of Dr. Henry Abrams, a Princeton ophthalmologist, who had agreed to measure Bradley's total field. Bradley rested his chin in the middle of a device called a perimeter, and Dr. Abrams began asking when he could see a small white dot as it was slowly brought around from behind him, from above, from below, and from either side. To make sure that Bradley wasn't, in effect, throwing hope passes, Dr. Abrams checked each point three times before plotting it on a chart. There was a chart for each eye, and both charts had irregular circles printed on them, representing the field of vision that a typical perfect eye could be expected to have. Dr. Abrams explained as he worked that these printed circles were logical rather than experimentally established extremes, and that in his experience the circles he had plotted to represent the actual vision fields of his patients had without exception fallen inside the circles printed on the charts. When he finished plotting Bradley's circles, the one for each eye was larger than the printed model and, in fact, ran completely outside it.

With both eyes open and looking straight ahead, Bradley sees a hundred and ninety-five degrees on the horizontal and about seventy degrees straight down, or about fifteen and five degrees more, respectively, than what is officially considered perfection. Most surprising, however, is what he can see above him. Focussed horizontally, the typical perfect eye, according to the chart, can see about forty-seven degrees upward. Bradley can see seventy degrees upward. This no doubt explains why he can stare at the floor while he is waiting for lobbed passes to arrive from above. Dr. Abrams said that he doubted whether a person who tried to expand his peripheral vision through exercises could succeed, but he was fascinated to learn that when Bradley was a young boy he tried to do just that. As he walked down the main street of Crystal City, for example, he would keep his eyes focussed straight ahead and try to identify objects in the windows of stores he was passing. For all this, however, Bradley cannot see behind himself. Much of the court and, thus, a good deal of the action are often invisible to a basketball player, so he needs more than good eyesight. He needs to know how to function in the manner of a blind man as well. When, say, four players are massed in the middle of things behind Bradley, and it is inconvenient for him to look around, his hands reach back and his fingers move rapidly from shirt to shirt or hip to hip. He can read the defense as if he were reading Braille.

Bradley's optical endowments notwithstanding, Coach van Breda Kolff agrees with him that he is "not a great physical player," and goes on to say, "Others can run faster and jump higher. The difference between Bill and other basketball players is self-discipline." The two words that Bradley repeats most often when he talks about basketball are "discipline" and "concentration," and through the exercise of both he has made himself an infectious example to younger players. "Concentrate!" he keeps shouting to himself when he is practicing on his own. His capacity for self-discipline is so large that it is almost funny. For example, he was a bit shocked when the Olympic basketball staff advised the Olympic basketball players to put in one hour of practice a day during the summer, because he was already putting in two hours a day—often in ninety-five-degree temperatures, with his feet squishing in sneakers that had become so wet that he sometimes skidded and crashed to the floor. His creed, which he picked up from Ed Macauley, is "When you are not practicing, remember, someone somewhere is practicing, and when you meet him he will win."

He also believes that the conquest of pain is essential to any seriously sustained athletic endeavor. In 1963, he dressed for a game against Harvard although he had a painful foot injury. Then, during the pre-game warmup, it bothered him so much that he decided to give up, and he started for the bench. He changed his mind on the way, recalling that a doctor had told him that his foot, hurt the night before at Dartmouth, was badly bruised but was not in danger of further damage. If he sat down, he says, he would have lowered his standards, for he believes that "there has never been a great athlete who did not know what pain is." So he played the game. His heavily taped foot went numb during the first ten minutes, but his other faculties seemed to sharpen in response to the handicap. His faking quickened to make up for his reduced speed, and he scored thirty-two points, missing only five shots during the entire evening.

How Bradley acquired these criteria and became a superstar is not what interests people in basketball. If they think about it at all, they wonder *why* he did it. "Where did this kid get his dedication?" Macauley asks. "Why did he decide to make the sacrifices?" The pattern of his life seems to provide an answer to the question, beginning with the fact that he used the sport as a way to get to know other boys, for he was an only child.

Crystal City, which was once an active river port, now has a population of about four thousand, with a preponderance of Italians, Greeks, French, and Slavs, and a considerable proportion of blacks. Its principal street, Mississippi Avenue, is paved with red brick and overhung with the limbs of oak and tulip trees. Although the town is fully incorporated, its people see it as a collection of unofficial subdivisions, various neighborhoods being known as Crystal Valley, Crystal Terrace, Crystal Heights, Old Town, Downtown, Crystal Village, and North Crystal. A stranger arriving at night and hearing talk of all these areas might well believe he was in a sprawling megalopolis. In reality, the town has a three-man police force; it has one factory, an enormous one that makes plate glass and that indirectly gave the town its name; and it has one bank president, and one bank president's son.

The Bradleys live on Taylor Avenue, behind picture windows that look out on the Grace Presbyterian Church, across the street, whose ample churchyard forms a kind of town common. Elsewhere in Crystal City, weeds sometimes grow at forty-five-degree angles out of the clefts where the streets meet the curbstones, and property owners tend to resign themselves to having brown lawns in summer, but in and around the churchyard everything is trim, immaculate, and green.

When Warren Bradley, Bill's father, goes to work in the morning, he walks halfway around the churchyard to the Crystal City State Bank, where, according to his wife, he "started out as a penny shiner" in 1921. His father had died in 1910, when he was nine, and he had been able to complete only one year at Crystal City High School before going to work, first as a ticketseller for the Missouri & Illinois Railroad and later as a yard clerk for the Frisco Line. "The feel of money seemed to appeal to me," he says in explaining his switchover to banking. Sixteen years after joining the bank, he became its president. In the meantime, he compensated for his abbreviated education by reading on his own, and although his son is a Rhodes Scholar, he is still the most incisive and articulate member of the family. He cares about

politics with a studious passion and, ignoring the possible effect of his beliefs on his business, is a conten-
tious Republican in a town full of Democrats.

He is ordinarily a reserved man, and he has a soft
voice, but when something worth reacting to comes
along, he reacts, and often bluntly. Four years ago,
when his son was under very heavy recruitment pressure from college coaches, Mr. Bradley was disturbed
by all the attention his family was getting, because he
didn't think that basketball was that important. One
day, a man walked into the Crystal City State Bank
without an appointment and asked Mr. Bradley's
secretary to say that Adolph Rupp had come to call.
Rupp, known throughout basketball as The Baron,
has for thirty-five years been the coach at the University of Kentucky. He works more meticulously and
expensively than any other coach, having movies
taken at every practice, which he studies each morning as if he were John Huston going over the daily
rushes. He once drove Artur Rubinstein out of his
gym because the pianist, preparing for a concert, disturbed the concentration of the Kentucky Wildcats.
He has won more than seven hundred games while

losing only a hundred and forty-five, and he once won three national championships in four years. Rupp still gets indignant when he remembers that Mr. Bradley was too busy to see him immediately. Rupp had to wait an hour and a half.

Thanks to a noteworthy stamina of spirit, Mr. Bradley has overcome the inconveniences of having calcified arthritis of the lower spine, which has made him unable to bend over for nearly twenty-five years. He uses long wooden tweezers to pick up objects from the floor. He was almost forty when he married Susan Crowe, who was a graduate of Central College, in Fayette, Missouri, and was then teaching in a junior high school in St. Louis. She grew up near Herculaneum, a town a few miles up the river from Crystal City, and she played interscholastic basketball for Herculaneum High School—a bit of family history that amuses her son. She is five feet seven, and her husband is six feet one and a half. What Bill Bradley calls the luck of being the son of these parents arises from the marked differences in their personalities. If Mr. Bradley is a contemplative man with "an enlightened disinterest," in his son's words, in

regard to athletic pinnacles, Mrs. Bradley is an out-
going and amiably competitive woman of immense
dynamism. Her father, a coffee salesman, was a big,
rough man who could bend spikes in his hands, could
do six things at once, liked to tell jokes all night, and
was proud of a mark on his forehead where a stallion
had once bit him. Mrs. Bradley, who is full of high
spirits herself, spends her life doing things for other
people, except when she's on the links at the Joachim
Country Club. She says that she couldn't care less
who wins and who loses at any game, but she usually
wins, and she has been club champion. Edward
Rapp, the principal of the Crystal City High School,
grew up with Mrs. Bradley and watched with interest as she raised her son. "Susie knew what kind of a
son she wanted, and by dint of determination she has
him," Rapp says. She herself says, "I wanted a Christian upright citizen, and I thought the best way to
begin was by promoting things that would interest a
little boy." She always had a busy program planned
for him, full of golf lessons, swimming lessons, piano
lessons, French lessons, trumpet lessons, dancing lessons, and tennis lessons.

When Bradley went out on his own, he sometimes encountered attitudes that disconcerted him. The churchyard was a favorite site with boys in the town for pickup games of tackle football. Crossing the street with the idea of joining in, he would sometimes hear the other boys say something like "Oh, here comes the banker's son," in a tone that made it clear enough that they did not want him. "This was something that hurt me in a very personal way," he says. "They would not judge me for what I was." In one form or another, the stigma of being the banker's son remained with him for some years, and it made him feel that he had more of a need to prove himself than others did.

He gradually became tolerated in the churchyard football games, whereupon he displayed another peculiarity, which no one really minded. All little boys playing tackle do so with the understanding that they are not really themselves but small and temporary incarnations of the greatest playing stars. The other boys in the churchyard would announce their names one by one, all of them claiming to be stalwarts of the University of Missouri or some other midwestern school. Bradley, for his part, always told them he was Dick Kazmaier, of Princeton, who in the early fifties won the Heisman Trophy as the outstanding college football player in the United States. Today, Bradley wears on his basketball uniform at Princeton the number 42, which is the number that Kazmaier used in football.

Bradley first played basketball, in the Crystal City Y.M.C.A., when he was nine years old. "It was just for something to do," he recalls. When his mother saw that he was interested in the game, she put a basket on the side of the garage so that he could play with his fellow Cub Scouts, to whom she was den mother. Each year, however, the seasonal fever for basketball had just begun to rise when it was time to go to Palm Beach. This was a recurrent frustration, for at the Palm Beach Private School, which he attended, soccer, fencing, and boxing were the major sports. When the school day ended at two, Bradley would hurry out past the limousines that were picking up his classmates, run back to the hotel where his parents stayed, go to his room, and reach under his bed for his basketball—an odd item to take along on a trip to Florida. With a series of tympanic thumps, he would dribble out of the room, across the lobby and the street, and along the sidewalks, under the columnar palms. There was a public schoolyard several blocks away with a basket in it, and he played there every day. Now and then, a few tatterdemalions from West Palm Beach came to the playground, and he befriended them eagerly. "Basketball was a way to get to know guys," he says. But usually he was alone. This, as much as any place, was where the fundamental narcotic of basketball entered his system. He can remember quite vividly how he felt about the game and about himself as he played it, and once, when I asked him about it, he closed his eyes and said, "What attracted me was the sound of the swish, the sound of the dribble, the feel of going up in the air. You don't need eight others, like in baseball. You don't need any brothers or sisters. Just you. I wonder what the guys are doing back home. I'd like to be there, but it's as much fun here, because I'm playing. It's getting dark. I have to go back for dinner. I'll shoot a couple more. Feels good. A couple more."

Toward the end of seventh grade, Bill told his

father he wanted to stay in Crystal City in future winters, and his father consented. The Bradley house then became the community center, for Bill had things that the other boys didn't have—television in his bedroom, for example, and a pinball machine in the basement. On the inside of his bedroom door he had a basketball net, and when the weather was bad outdoors he would get down on his knees—he was six feet three when he was in the eighth grade—and play against boys his own age, two at a time. Conditions outside had to be pretty unsavory before that happened, though; he and his friends played around the outdoor basket in gloves, if necessary, and at night, under floodlights. Gradually, Bradley's back yard evolved into a basketball court nearly as good as Princeton's. "Our yard wasn't for the purpose of raising grass," his father recalls. "There was no grass in it at all." This was because they had a macadam surface put over it, flat and smooth, around the steel pole supporting a fan-shaped backboard, whose hoop was exactly ten feet above the ground. There must be at least five million back-yard baskets in the United States, yet it is possible to search through a whole

community without finding more than half a dozen
at the regulation height.

Bradley's high-school basketball coach, Arvel Popp
(pronounced "Pope"), says that he began cultivating
Bradley when the boy was still in grade school. What
Popp was mainly cultivating, however, was a football
player, because at that time, at least, he was a football
coach first and a basketball coach second. Before
Bradley reached high-school age, Popp told him, "I'm
going to make you into the finest end who ever
played for the University of Missouri." Bradley
therefore incurred double jeopardy when, entering
high school, he showed no interest in football. He
had to do what he could to dispel gossip that he was
chicken, and he had to prove himself as a basketball
player to Coach Popp, for Popp was not interested in
having boys on his basketball team who didn't play
football.

If basketball was going to enable Bradley to make
friends, to prove that a banker's son is as good as the
next fellow, to prove that he could do without being
the greatest-end-ever at Missouri, to prove that he was
not chicken, and to live up to his mother's champion-

ship standards, and if he was going to have some moments left over to savor his delight in the game, he obviously needed considerable practice, so he borrowed keys to the gym and set a schedule for himself that he adhered to for four full years—in the school year, three and a half hours every day after school, nine to five on Saturday, one-thirty to five on Sunday, and, in the summer, about three hours a day. He put ten pounds of lead slivers in his sneakers, set up chairs as opponents and dribbled in slalom fashion around them, and wore eyeglass frames that had a piece of cardboard taped to them so that he could not see the floor, for a good dribbler never looks at the ball. Aboard the Queen Elizabeth on a trip to Europe one summer, he found that the two longitudinal corridors on C Deck, Tourist Class, were each about four hundred and fifty feet long, making nine hundred feet in all, or ten times the length of a basketball floor. This submarine palaestra became the world's finest training area in two respects. It was not only the longest gym on earth, it was also the narrowest, measuring forty-eight inches across. The width was ideal for the practice of dribbling, since it tended to bunch the opposition, or fellow-passengers, who got used to hearing the approaching thump-thump of the basketball, and to seeing what appeared to be a six-foot-five-inch lunatic come bearing down upon them with a device on his face that cut off much of his vision.

Coach Popp, as it turned out, was less inflexible than his reputation suggested. After his varsity basketball team lost its first four games, he decided to put a freshman—Bradley—in his lineup, for the second time ever, and after that the Crystal City Hornets won sixteen out of twenty-one. The older boys on the team resented Bradley's presence a little, and were also suspicious of him, because he would sometimes use the waiting time in the locker room before a game to bring out a textbook and study. They passed to him fairly infrequently in that first year, but, largely as a result of vacuuming rebounds, he averaged twenty points a game. The resentment arose from the natural tendency of high-school boys to give a great deal of importance to seniority, and by his third year it was gone. Once an anomaly, he was now a model. One of his teammates of those years, Sam La Presta, has recalled, "Bill did what he did by hard work. Everyone looked up to him. He was sort of inspirational. Basketball was one-millionth of what he had to offer."

At Princeton, Bradley has become such an excellent basketball player that it is necessary to look beyond college basketball to find a standard that will put him in perspective. The standard's name is Oscar Robertson, of the Cincinnati Royals, who is the finest basketball player yet developed.

Robertson, who is known in basketball as The O, stands out among all professionals for the same reason that Bradley stands out among all amateurs. Other players have certain individual skills that are sharper, but Bradley and Robertson are accomplished in every aspect of the game. To make a detailed comparison between Bradley and Robertson as they are now, Robertson is a better rebounder and a better defensive player, notwithstanding the defensive performance that Bradley gave in an exhibition game last fall between the Olympic team and the Royals, when he held Robertson to eleven points. Bradley is as good a

passer as Robertson, and they are about even in dribbling, too. Going hard for the basket, Robertson is a
better driver. "When I watch Robertson," Bradley
says, "I just stand with my mouth wide open. There
are so many things he does that I could never do in a
hundred years. I could never feel confident, the way
he can, that I could shoot jump shots against anybody
at all. He's the best basketball player alive." Bradley
adds that one of the big differences between his abilities and Robertson's is that The O has better body
control and is more deceptive when he moves. Bradley, for his part, has a greater variety of shots than
Robertson, and is, in general, a more accurate shooter.
As Bradley notes, however, he doesn't have the same
jump shot. Bradley is merely outstanding with his
jumper. But no one has a jump shot like Robertson's
—frozen in the air, with his back arched and his
hands behind his head, where the ball is totally pro-
tected until he sends it into the basket. Bradley's
jump shot is released, more conventionally, from just
above his head. The O's jump shot is literally "un-
stoppable"—the most intoxicating adjective in basket-

ball. If Bradley does enough shooting this year, he
may become the second-highest scorer in the records
of college basketball, but he will still be about four
hundred points under the final count that Robertson
left behind him at the University of Cincinnati. Robertson and his Royals teammate Jerry Lucas, who
played for Ohio State, are the only two basketball
players who have been included on the *Sporting News*
All-American team, which is picked by the professional scouts, in all three of their college basketball
seasons. This year, barring the unforeseen, Bradley
will become the third. Among Bradley's Olympic
teammates was U.C.L.A.'s Walt Hazzard, now a Los
Angeles Laker, who, like Robertson, is black, and
he passed along to Bradley a compliment of unforget-
table magnitude. "Where I come from," Hazzard
told Bradley, "you are known as The White O."
  With all his analyses of its mechanics, Bradley may
have broken his game down into its components, but
he has reassembled it so seamlessly that all the parts,
and also his thousands of hours of practice, are con-
cealed. He is as fluidly graceful as any basketball

player I have ever seen. Quite apart from the excitement produced by the scoreboard, a spectator cannot
help feeling a considerable elation as he watches
Bradley accomplish his fakes and moves and shots.
He does it all with a floating economy of motion and
a beguiling offhandedness that appeal to the imagina-
tion. Many basketball players, outstanding ones included, have a tendency to be rather tastelessly rococo
in their style, and Bradley stands out in contrast to
them because he adorns nothing that he does. When
a game is won beyond doubt, and Bradley leaves the
court with three or four minutes to go, the coach of
the opposing team has sometimes halted play to walk
down to the Princeton bench and shake his hand.
The coach doesn't do this just because Bradley has
scored thirty-five or forty points but because he has
done it so uncompromisingly well.

This season, in the course of a tournament held
during the week after Christmas, Bradley took part
in a game that followed extraordinarily the pattern
of his game against St. Joseph's. Because the stakes

were higher, it was a sort of St. Joseph's game to the third power. Whereas St. Joseph's had been the best team in the East, Princeton's opponent this time was Michigan, the team that the Associated Press and the United Press International had rated as the best college team of all.

The chance to face Michigan represented to Bradley the supreme test of his capability as a basketball player. As he saw it, any outstanding player naturally hopes to be a member of the country's No. 1 team, but if that never happens, the next-best thing is to be tested against the No. 1 team. And the Michigan situation seemed even more important to him because, tending as he sometimes does to question his own worth, he was uncomfortably conscious that a committee had picked him for the Olympic team, various committees had awarded him his status as an All-American, and, for that matter, committees had elected him a Rhodes Scholar. Michigan, he felt, would provide an exact measurement of him as an athlete.

The height of the Michigan players averages six

feet five, and nearly every one of them weighs over two hundred pounds. Smoothly experienced, both as individuals and as a coördinated group, they have the appearance, the manner, and the assurance of a professional team. One of them, moreover, is Cazzie Russell, who, like Bradley, was a consensus All-American last year. For a couple of days before the game, the sports pages of the New York newspapers were crammed with headlines, articles, and even cartoons comparing Bradley and Russell, asking which was the better player, and looking toward what one paper called the most momentous individual confrontation in ten years of basketball.

One additional factor—something that meant relatively little to Bradley—was that the game was to be played in Madison Square Garden. Bradley had never played in the Garden, but, because he mistrusts metropolitan standards, he refused to concede that the mere location of the coming test meant anything at all. When a reporter asked him how he felt about appearing there, he replied, "It's just like any other place. The baskets are ten feet high."

Bradley now says that he prepared for the Michigan game as he had prepared for no other. He slept for twelve hours, getting up at noon. Then, deliberately, he read the New York newspapers and absorbed the excited prose which might have been announcing a prizefight: FESTIVAL DUEL: BILL BRADLEY VS. CAZZIE RUSSELL . . . CAZZIE—BRADLEY: KEY TEST . . . BRADLEY OR CAZZIE? SHOWDOWN AT HAND . . . BILL BRADLEY OF PRINCETON MEETS CAZZIE RUSSELL OF MICHIGAN TONIGHT AT THE GARDEN!! This exposure to the newspapers had the effect he wanted; he developed chills, signifying a growing stimulation within him. During most of the afternoon, when any other player in his situation would probably have been watching television, shooting pool, or playing ping-pong or poker—anything to divert the mind— Bradley sat alone and concentrated on the coming game, on the components of his own play, and on the importance to him and his team of what would occur. As much as anything, he wanted to prove that an Ivy League team could be as good as any other team. Although no newspaper gave Princeton even the slightest chance of winning, Bradley did not just hope to do well himself—he intended that Princeton should win.

Just before he went onto the court, Bradley scrubbed his hands with soap and water, as he always does before a game, to remove any accumulated skin oil and thus increase the friction between his fingers and the ball. When the game was forty-two seconds old, he hit a jump shot and instantly decided, with a rush of complete assurance of a kind that sometimes comes over an athlete in action, that a victory was not only possible but probable.

Michigan played him straight, and he played Michigan into the floor. The performance he delivered had all the depth and variation of theoretical basketball, each move being perfectly executed against able opposition. He stole the ball, he went back door, he threw unbelievable passes. He reversed away from the best defenders in the Big Ten. He held his own man to one point. He played in the backcourt, in the post, and in the corners. He made long set shots, and hit jump shots from points so far behind the basket that he had to start them from arm's length in order to clear the backboard. He tried a hook shot on the dead run and hit that, too. Once, he found himself in a corner of the court with two Michigan players, both taller than he, pressing in on him shoulder to shoulder. He parted them with two rapid fakes—a move of the ball and a move of his head—and leaped up between them to sink a twenty-two-foot jumper. The same two players soon cornered him again. The fakes were different the second time, but the result was the same. He took a long stride between them and went up into the air, drifting forward, as they collided behind him, and he hit a clean shot despite the drift.

Bradley, playing at the top of his game, drew his teammates up to the best performances they could give, too, and the Princeton team as a whole outplayed Michigan. The game, as it had developed, wasn't going to be just a close and miraculous Princeton victory, it was going to be a rout. But, with Princeton twelve points ahead, Bradley, in the exuberance of sensing victory, made the mistake of playing close defense when he did not need to, and when he was too tired to do it well. He committed his fifth personal foul with four minutes and thirty-seven seconds to go, and had to watch the end of the game from the bench. As he sat down, the twenty thousand spectators stood up and applauded him for some three minutes. It was, as the sportswriters and the Garden management subsequently agreed, the most clamorous ovation ever given a basketball player, amateur or professional, in Madison Square Garden. Bradley's duel with Russell had long since become incidental. Russell scored twenty-seven points and showed his All-American calibre, but during the long applause the announcer on the Garden loudspeakers impulsively turned up the volume and said, "Bill Bradley, one of the greatest players ever to play in Madison Square Garden, scored forty-one points."

After he left the court—joining two of his teammates who had also fouled out—Michigan overran Princeton, and won the game by one basket. Bradley ultimately was given the trophy awarded to the most valuable player in the tournament, but his individual recognition meant next to nothing to him, because of Princeton's defeat.

It had become fully apparent, however, that Brad-

ley would be remembered as one of college basketball's preeminent stars. He had ratified his reputation
—not through his point total nearly so much as
through his total play.

3. Ivy League

When Bradley had an off-night, as he sometimes did, it seldom just descended on him at random. Generally, a cold performance would seem to be related to his mood and outlook of the moment, and if he was preoccupied with problems outside of basketball, the preoccupation was likely to show through in the way he played. He could leave basketball behind him when he went to the library, but he apparently could not always forget his work when he went to the gym. Sometimes, this produced startling and amusing reversals of form.

Princeton's first 1965 Ivy League game, for example, was played on January 8 against Yale at Princeton, and Bradley went into it feeling dismal in several ways. He had stayed up the night before until two a.m., writing a difficult paper, which was still unfinished. He had two other papers with imminent deadlines and three final examinations in first-semester courses approaching closely, and he seemed to be feeling sorry for himself. His play on the court reflected his gloomy state of mind. He missed every shot he tried during the first half, free throws excepted, going zero for eight from the floor. Moreover, he missed all but three of his shots in the second half. Yale, not a memorable team, was electrified with sudden ambition, and the game ended in a tie. In the overtime, Bradley won the game for Princeton by scoring seven points in five minutes. Because of those seven, he had scored twenty-one points in all, but it was still the worst performance he would ever give as a college player.

Too tired to do anything else, he went to his room after the game and slept for nine hours. The next morning, working in the library, he found that he had been much closer to the end of the paper he was writing than he had thought. He finished it, and, on the same day, found that the deadline for one of his other course papers had been extended. Princeton played its second Ivy League game, against Brown, that night. Rested, relaxed, and with a sense of unexpected survival, Bradley was so exuberant that the change in his mood was noticeable even in the way he warmed up. In the game, he scored thirty-eight points, hitting sixteen out of twenty-one, or seventy-six percent of his shots.

Some of his cold moments were not so easy to fathom, however, an example of which occurred a week later. One of his hopes, as Princeton's captain, was that he could lead his teammates through a season without defeat in the Ivy League, something that no Ivy League team had done for fourteen years. The outcome of the next two games, he said, would determine if this could be done, because they would be played on January 15 and 16, near the end of the yearly time of heavy academic pressure, nervousness, and sleepless cramming for examinations. Pronounced differences that may later show up between Ivy League teams tend to be flattened during this period, and games played away from home are particularly difficult to win. Bradley felt certain that if Princeton could get past Columbia, in New York on the 15th, and Cornell, at Ithaca on the 16th, it would not lose again in its regular season.

Columbia went down without incident, except that in the course of scoring forty-one points, Bradley scored the two thousandth point of his college career. There was an official time-out for a kind of ceremony in which he was presented with the ball. Only sixteen other players in college basketball history had ever reached that level, many of them in four years of competition.

The team moved toward Ithaca that night, by bus, through a blizzard that caused a delay. They stopped at Endicott, New York, at four a.m. The following evening, when the game was supposed to begin, Cornell's Barton Hall was jammed beyond its capacity and all open areas around the court were filled with people so close together that they appeared to be crowding in to watch an important rooster fight rather than a basketball game. Meanwhile a busload of Upper New York State Princeton alumni and their wives, all with tickets and high expectations of seeing Bradley play, had been stopped outside somewhere and told that they could not proceed because there was no more room for anyone. When van Breda Kolff heard this, he said his team would not play until the Princeton alumni were inside the hall and in their seats. For one thing, his sister was on the bus. The game started about twenty minutes late with the alumni installed. Ordinarily a slow bus trip and an irritating delay would not be enough to throw Bradley off his game, and he was not particularly worried about his exams, so he could not understand, after the game had begun, why he couldn't hit his shots. From the low post, he took a three-foot hook shot, usually an automatic score, but it hit the rim and rebounded away. He missed driving lay-up shots and short jump shots, in addition, of course, to all the shots he was missing from greater distances. Later, he said that he had never felt colder. During the first half, he hit two shots out of seventeen.

The Princeton team around him would not become a five-part, five-man coordinated unit until the middle of February, and when Bradley was cold, the whole group, in that part of the season, tended to be disorganized and weak. With about fourteen minutes to go, Princeton was sixteen points behind, and the game seemed clearly lost. "I thought of everything I could possibly be doing wrong," Bradley remembered later. "My arms. My eyes. All I could think was that maybe I was too worried about the man."

The man was Dave Bliss, a solidly built, good athlete, who, as Cornell's best defensive player, had been chasing Bradley around for three years and at last appeared to be catching him. "O.K., Bliss," Bradley remembers saying to himself, "the picnic's over now." He took a pass, reversed, jumped high over Bliss's arms and sank a nineteen-foot jumper. In the next few exchanges, he hit another shot, and another shot, and another, and another. He had scored ten points in the first half. He scored thirty more in the second. With one minute to go, Princeton was ahead by one point and went into a stall merely to close out the game. One of Bradley's teammates was fouled. He missed the foul shot, and Cornell got the ball. With a couple of seconds to go, a Cornell player hit a jump shot and dramatically saved the game for Cornell.

That was the one Ivy game that Princeton was

going to lose, but the *Daily Princetonian* (the undergraduate newspaper), never notable either for its
prescience or for its confidence in Princeton teams,
wrote that "Princeton still plays the same muddle-
shoot-and-give-the-ball-to-Bradley game, and still gets
beaten when an opponent catches the Tiger All-
American on an off night. . . . The dreams of national
ranking are fairly dead now. . . . As a matter of fact,
as things stand now, Princeton may need luck to win
the Ivy title everyone took for granted."

This last prediction almost at once proved to have
some substance, although not because of anything
that Princeton's team, in itself, lacked. After the two-
week examination period, Princeton played a game
against Pennsylvania in Philadelphia in which, for
the first half at least, it appeared that the winning
side was going to be the one which had any players at
all in the game at the end. The rules of basketball are
such that if they were ever literally interpreted the
referees would call enough fouls in any game to elim-
inate everyone on both squads two or three times
over. No sport, therefore, is more difficult to officiate,
since the referee's judgment is infinitely more im-

portant than his vision, and the fairness of the outcome depends on the consistency and balance of the
referee's decisions rather than on any set of inflexible rules. Basketball players are always all over one
another, elbowing, hooking, feeling for position,
crashing shoulders, ramming one another in the chest
if they get annoyed at overplayed defense—and there
simply isn't room enough in the central playing area
for everyone to avoid contact in the way that the rules
suggest.

All teams once in a while have to suffer through
poor officiating, because even outstanding officials
have off nights, just as outstanding players do. In the
Princeton-Pennsylvania game in Philadelphia, the
coaches of both teams were forced to pull first-team
players out of the game during the first half because
the referees were calling about two hundred and fifty
percent of the usual and expectable number of fouls.
It appeared that Princeton was going to lose Bradley
and two other starters, and Pennsylvania had nothing
to rejoice about because their better players were on
the way out, too. While warming up for the second
half, Bradley was so discouraged that he had tears in

his eyes. In an attempt to cope with the problem, van Breda Kolff decided to have his team play a zone defense during the second half, even though, in his opinion, a zone defense is a sign of weakness, and neither he nor his predecessor at Princeton had ever used one. Almost every time a Penn player had driven for the basket during the first half, a foul had been called against a Princeton player. The zone automatically stopped Penn's driving game. Bradley and his teammates simply held their hands in the air and went for rebounds after Penn would shoot from the outside. The Philadelphia *Bulletin* headline the next day said, "Bradley's 36 Points Down Penn, 83-72." Van Breda Kolff's zone defense, which had appeared at first to be a hopeless bolt for cover, had in the end proved to be a master's move.

Having defeated Brown at Princeton, Princeton now went to Providence to do so again—in a dull and dispirited game which enraged van Breda Kolff. At the end of the first half, when the score should have been about fifty to twenty-five, Princeton was scarcely in the lead. Bradley had hit sixty percent of his shots, but he had only tried five, so he was hardly scoring at all. The rest of the Princeton players were playing the game as if they had pressing appointments elsewhere. Boys on the Princeton bench noticed in the grandstands the members of the basketball team of Providence College. Not having a game of their own that night, they had come to see Bradley and his team. Providence was the only undefeated basketball team in the United States at the time. As spectators, they seemed skeptical about the stature of what they had come to see. At any rate, they were clutching themselves as if to keep from falling off their seats while having spasms of mirth and disbelief.

Van Breda Kolff walked into the locker room during the half, picked up a piece of chalk, and threw it against the blackboard so hard that it disintegrated into a puff of dust. He was violently sucking air into his mouth and breathing it out in what might have been flame. He picked up another piece of chalk and wrote at the top of the blackboard, in huge letters, the word "FOOD." Then, with equally large lettering, he wrote "SLEEP," "GIRLS," "STUDIES." Far down the blackboard, in extremely small letters, he wrote, "Basketball." Then he bent over and crimped himself

up and produced an even tinier hieroglyph—"winning."

"Nobody wants to win!" he bellowed. But his team
was winning in spite of itself.

Bradley was hurt the following afternoon, and his
injuries, if they had been only slightly more exten-
sive, would have finished his season. As it was, he
was unable to practice with his team for two weeks.
He appeared in four games during that time, because
his presence on the court, as many coaches had already observed, was enough to stifle the ambitions of
other teams. But he had lost all of his effective speed,
much of his ability to get up in the air, and nearly
all of his moves that depended on his legs—notably
the reverse pivot, which was vital to him but which
disappeared from his game until a month later, when
he was playing in the national tournament.

He had collided with a Yale player and had dam-
aged both his right knee and his right thigh. He felt
considerable pain in the cartilage area and, as he put
it later, "my thigh was immediately stone." Soon he
developed fever, chills, and dizziness. Even before

they had returned to Princeton, his coach and his teammates realized that, for a time at least, they were going to have to do pretty much without him.

This realization, both Bradley and van Breda Kolff feel, was the key to the outcome of the season. It is possible for one superstar, in any league or conference, to patch together a league title pretty much on his own, with a loss here and there, but with enough victories to make the difference. It takes a team to go anywhere at all in the national championships, and during the next two weeks Princeton's other basketball players became a thoroughgoing, monokinetic team.

One reason why this crystallization had not occurred earlier is that three of the first six were sophomores, and two months of varsity competition is hardly time enough for sophomores to become grooved and settled, particularly if they happen to be playing with a senior who is averaging over thirty points a game, and on whom they will naturally depend to an unbalancing degree. Playing together during those two weeks, Princeton's other players discovered themselves—and there was much to find. Bradley's team had considerable talent, far more than was realized by anyone at the time, themselves included.

Ed Hummer, one of the sophomores, had been a high school All-American in Arlington, Virginia. All season, Van Breda Kolff kept him on the bench during the first ten minutes or so, alternating him with Robbie Brown, another sophomore, or, when he needed a lot of height, taking someone else out and sending Hummer and Brown under the boards together. Hummer, at the time, was six feet six inches tall, and Brown was six feet nine. Both were taller than Bradley. Hummer, with good jumping ability and many well-practiced moves, seemed to be the player who would in following seasons become Princeton's high scorer. Van Breda Kolff used him as sixth man only as an offensive tactic—to have power coming off the bench.

Brown, whose father is the Director of Career and Study Services at Princeton (running a kind of personnel office which helps Princeton graduates and undergraduates find jobs), is a giant response to van Breda Kolff's prejudice that prep school boys can't play college basketball. Brown once played for Exeter.

He grew so rapidly that he left some energy behind, but van Breda Kolff played him a bit longer in each game than in the one before. With his height, his rebounding ability, and his defensive skill at blocking shots all over the center area, he could force other teams to do their shooting from the outside.

Actually, van Breda Kolff had a player from Andover as well—a short, fast, quick-handed back-court man and good shooter named Bill Kingston, who was one of Bradley's roommates and who, after graduation, went to Tunisia with the Peace Corps. Kingston and another senior named Don Roth, a football halfback from Bethesda, Maryland, constituted a kind of medical unit, going into games when the first six seemed to be psychologically dishevelled, steadying down the play, stealing the ball from the opposition, and often changing the chemistry of the game. Kingston was a fair basketball player who had made himself into a good one through practice and complete dedication. Roth was less a basketball player or a football player than he was a general athlete—naturally smart in any athletic situation, and glib and funny as well, often making his teammates laugh when they particularly needed to. He never understood Bradley's constant passing off. When Roth was in the game, he was constantly feeding the ball to Bradley. After all, that was where the points were.

Gary Walters, a sophomore from Reading, Pennsylvania, was clearly going to become one of the most able players who had ever worn a Princeton uniform —small and fast, with a long and deadly set shot, a good sense of defensive play, and an ability to drive through a whole team to score with a running hook. Even in his first season he was playing heady basketball, and, being a particularly skillful dribbler, he could bring the ball up the floor against a press, taking some of the pressure off Bradley, who had occasionally functioned as a backcourt man and a forward at the same time.

Don Rodenbach, of Bethlehem, Pennsylvania, playing his second season with Bradley, had played for a high school team which used a zone defense. Learning the man-to-man strategies quickly, he had become an outstanding defensive player, as he had demonstrated when he covered Cazzie Russell in the holiday Michigan game. Rodenbach was trying to develop his ability to drive well for the basket. He already had a long outside jump shot that was pretty to watch and remarkably accurate.

Bob Haarlow, who eventually was elected captain of the team for the following year, had proved himself to be an unspectacular basketball player but an exceptional one. There was no paradox in that. Haarlow's game had long since become sound in all ways; he seemed to be a natively smart basketball player and he could do everything. He moved a little better without the ball than anyone else but Bradley. As a result, he got more of Bradley's passes than anyone else did. He was the second highest scorer. His father, General Manager of the Illinois Bell Telephone Company, was once a basketball star at Chicago, has since become Supervisor of Officials in the Big Ten, and has written a book on officiating.

During the two weeks that Bradley was unable to practice, Princeton was fortunate not to have any games of importance to play. There were four—two with Harvard and two with Dartmouth in a pair of home-and-home weekends—and neither Harvard nor

Dartmouth had much of a team. Bradley played in these games as a kind of figurehead, and his teammates' new attitude toward him seemed to be that they were humoring an old cripple, while they skillfully put down the opposition by themselves. Unable to break or cut with any kind of speed or deception, his leg bulging with pounds of tape, Bradley simply moved up and down, threw passes, accepted his diminished role, and enjoyed the brilliant displays of passing and shooting that his teammates put on. In the Harvard games, he scored twenty and twenty-four points, mainly on set shots from his wheel chair, and in one Dartmouth game he scored nineteen. In the other Dartmouth game, his point total seemed to belie his incapacitation. Hobbling around pathetically, he scored thirty-six points. I later asked him how this was possible, even against Dartmouth, which had a poor team. "They gave me fifteen-foot jumpers unmolested," he said. "You can hit those with a cast on your leg, not just a bandage." He had hit fourteen and missed eight, and he only played about three-quarters of the game.

With eight minutes to go in the same game, a

Princeton player named Ken Shank, of Lancaster, Pennsylvania, who had been on the bench from the outset, was sent into action. Even before he went onto the court, large segments of the crowd began to cheer for him with exaggerated enthusiasm, and banners bearing his name were unfurled in the grandstands. Undergraduate spectators raised streamers that said things like "We Love You, Kenny," "Ken Shank Fan Club," and "Shank for President." Another one said "Double Figures For Shank," and the intricate intention of this was that double figures for Ken Shank—scoring more than nine points in the few minutes remaining in the game—was such an incongruous idea that the mere suggestion of it would make the entire crowd shake with laughter.

Lots of people did laugh. Shank took it all with what should be classed as impassive good humor. He was used to it. He was a senior and had been on the basketball squad throughout his college days, playing only in the last moments of games which had long since been decided in Princeton's favor, as this one was. When he was sent in, the score was Princeton 86, Dartmouth 52. But while his particular value to the team had never been immediately apparent to the paying public, he had such value nonetheless. For four years, he had been the fellow whose exclusive responsibility in perhaps a thousand hours of practice had been to guard Bill Bradley. Bradley, for his part, had scored smoothly and without apparent difficulty against every kind of defense known in basketball, except Ken Shank. Every ripple of Bradley's manner as a basketball player was so well known to Shank that Bradley was often forced to be more inventive in practice than he had to be in games. Shank also possessed one remarkable physical characteristic. He could get up higher off the floor than any other player on the squad. Mindful of Shank's extraordinary spring and his highly specialized experience, Bradley, in practice scrimmages, knew that he had to be at his most precise or Shank would block his shots.

Shank was not a player whose appearance was athletically prepossessing. At least part of the reason why his followers in the stands were attracted to him was probably because he seemed to them to be an even more unlikely figure in a basketball uniform than they themselves would be. He appeared to be a

little too slim and fragile; the silhouette of his legs
did not suggest power; he wore tortoise-shell glasses;
and he had a fairly heavy beard that gave him a dark
chin and the look of a sleepless genius who had been
sent in from the library stacks rather than the bench.
And well he might have been, since he was a brilliant
student. As a basketball player, he scored more mod-
estly than he did when writing examinations, and the
spectators who so warmly adopted him at Princeton
were numbed with joy if he happened to score so
much as a single free throw. Waving their banners
and chanting "Shank! Shank! Shank!" they made him
a kind of mock-hero.

Every time his hands touched the ball, a roar went
up from his partisans. "Shoot! Shoot!", they called
out, even when he was at the wrong end of the court.
He had been in that particular game with Dartmouth
for about a minute when he actually did take a shot,
a long twenty-foot jumper that dropped cleanly into
the net. The applause was deafening. Shank soon hit
another jump shot, and the hall was in madness. In
succeeding moments, the figmented hero proved to
be a real one, performing in a manner that was quite

truly reminiscent of the great player he had been sparring with since 1961. He was fouled twice and he made both foul shots. He sent four more jump shots, some from fifteen and twenty feet out, plunging through the net. He missed only one shot he tried. Once, he even whirled and swept a hook shot toward the basket, and that dropped in, too. In no time at all, he had scored fourteen points, which made him the second highest Princeton scorer for the game. Because of his nearly perfect shooting, Princeton had surprisingly spurted to a finishing total of one hundred and three points. With twenty seconds to go, van Breda Kolff impulsively gave Shank the highest compliment he could possibly have given him. He sent Bill Bradley into the game as Shank's substitute. Shank left the floor with an unselfconscious smile illuminating his face. For well over a minute, the whole crowd stood up and applauded his performance, and the applause was now as genuine as it had ever been for Bradley himself.

For weeks, the team which had been leading the Ivy League was Cornell, and so much fever developed over the coming Cornell-Princeton game at

Princeton that closed-circuit television units were set up so that several thousand people could watch it from the grandstands in the swimming pool, and elsewhere on the Princeton campus. Bradley, in a curious maneuver, took his record player to the locker room and played two rock-n-roll songs—*Dancin' In The Street* and *The Boy From New York City*—over and over and over and over, all week before the game, imagining, one supposes, that the compounding sounds would carbonate the minds of his teammates and hop up their energies. The Cornell team, which had started the season powerfully, imploded toward the end, coming apart from the inside. By the time it arrived for the great game, it had already dropped two others, one to Yale and one to Pennsylvania.

"Nonetheless," Bradley said, looking back on it, "they had beaten us. We knew we were a better team than they were. We wanted to blow them off the court—and we did." Bradley played a solid, thirty-three-point game, but his role on the team was contributive and not commanding. The score was Princeton 107, Cornell 84. When it was over, Bradley rode to one basket on his teammates' shoulders and cut down the net. There was a kind of mop-up game left to be played with Pennsylvania, but the defeat of Cornell had mathematically settled the Ivy League Championship.

Near the end of the Pennsylvania game, Bradley took a pass in the right corner, turned, looked for the basket, and sent a seventeen-foot hook shot into the air. It was the last shot that he would ever take at Princeton, and, as basketball players like to say at the end of a practice, it was "one to quit on." The ball dropped in without touching the rim. Van Breda Kolff took him out of the game and for about five minutes—while play went on, points were scored, fouls were called, substitutions were made, and the game continued to its end—all the people in the grandstands stood up and applauded and went on applauding and watched Bradley on the bench rather than the action on the court. When it was over, an undergraduate went out onto the main floor and asked for silence. He said that Bradley had become so much a part of the world at large—a national figure at twenty-one, whose time was under siege by every sort of organization from the wire services to religious groups and the National Basketball Association—that the students of Princeton wanted to bring him back to Princeton, in a sense, and show him how he was regarded there. With the University's permission, they had removed the cast-iron pendulum from the center of the bell in Nassau Hall, the first building of the university, and they had mounted it on a base of finished walnut. Since before the American Revolution (and more than a century before basketball was even conceived), the bell has regulated the university day, marked the beginnings and ends of classes, and symbolized the university itself, as distinguished from any of its parts. Bradley often tossed aside the plaques, watches, and silver cups that were presented to him, with a look which suggested that he felt there was something a little absurd about it all, but he valued that piece of a bell even more than he did his Olympic gold medal. He waved good-bye, put it under his arm, and ran off the court. Needless to say, he had long since broken every individual scoring record which exists in the Ivy League. And he had already been named, by the wire services, basketball's Player of the Year. He would go with his team as far as he could in the national tournament, but that was the end at Princeton.

4. *Eastern Tournament*

The national tournament actually consists of five tournaments. The first four establish regional champions from the east to the far west. The four regional champions then meet for the tournament that decides, ultimately, the rankings which the wire services have been guessing at all season. Collectively known as the National Collegiate Championships, they are administered by the National Collegiate Athletic Association, which includes about six hundred colleges and fifteen thousand basketball players.

In the 1940's, when the N.C.A.A. tournament was less than ten years old, the National Invitation Tournament, a saturnalia held in New York at Madison Square Garden by The Metropolitan Intercollegiate

Basketball Association, was the most glamorous of the post-season tournaments and generally had the better teams. The winner of the National Invitation Tournament was regarded as more of a national champion than the actual, titular, national champion, or winner of the N.C.A.A. tournament. In 1950, the N.C.A.A. moved to change that situation, ruled that no team could compete in both tournaments, and, in effect, indicated that if a team were eligible for the N.C.A.A. tournament it had better play in it. Since then, the N.C.A.A. tournament has clearly been the major one, and the National Invitation Tournament has become a post-season showcase for good teams which did not make the N.C.A.A. grade.

Modern basketball—the age of the jump shot, of fifty-percent shooting, and of frequent three-figure scoring—began at about the same time that the N.C.A.A. tournament assumed its pre-eminence. By way of illustration, the dimensions of the modern era are outlined in the scoring records of the national championships, all of which have been set since 1950. In 1958, for example, in a regional consolation game between Cincinnati and Arkansas, Oscar Robertson scored fifty-six points to set the individual, single-game record. In the same game, Robertson hit twenty-one shots from the floor, establishing another record. Jerry West of West Virginia, the player from whom Bradley borrowed a part of his jump shot, scored one hundred and seventy-seven points over a five-game span, as his team went to, and ultimately lost in, the 1959 national finals. This tied a record set by Hal Lear of Temple, when his team finished third in the nation in 1956. Team records reflected the modern age, too. Loyola, for example, making its first move toward the national championship of 1963, defeated Tennessee Tech 111 to 42, scoring more points than any other team ever had in the national tournament.

In the Eastern Regionals, seven teams compete. The tournament always begins with a kind of preliminary elimination night, usually held in New York or Philadelphia, then the second round and the finals are held on an eastern university campus. Princeton's game with St. Joseph's in Bradley's sophomore year, played in Philadelphia, was a first round game. In 1964, after beating the Virginia Military Institute in the first round, Princeton lost to Connecticut, 52-50, in Raleigh. One of Bradley's teammates in 1965 evolved something which he called his "numerical progression theory" to inspire the team to new heights: since the team had been losing one less game in the Ivy League and winning one more game in the national tournament each year, it seemed to follow that in 1965 they were going to win their first two N.C.A.A. games. Throughout the modern era, no Ivy League team had ever gone beyond the second round of the regional play-offs. In fact, only Dartmouth had ever won more than one game.

Six teams went to Philadelphia for the first round —Connecticut, winner of the Yankee Conference; St. Joseph's, winner of the Middle Atlantic Conference; West Virginia, winner of the Southern Conference; Penn State and Providence, which do not belong to leagues or conferences and were at-large selections by the N.C.A.A.; and Princeton. Princeton's opponent was Penn State, which had won twenty games and lost three, and was famous for its zone defense. While he was warming up for the game, Bradley felt just right. His knee brace was finally gone. He was hitting one warm-up shot after another from all over the court. He went over to the sideline and said to Van Breda Kolff, "Boy, I hope I play the way I feel."

At about that moment, one of Princeton's players lost a contact lens and the procedure of the warm-up was interrupted for nearly five minutes while Princeton players got down on their hands and knees looking for it. Eventually, some of them lay down flat on the floor to squint along the individual boards. Bradley, standing beside van Breda Kolff, began to shift his arms restlessly and look disgusted with the whole farcical scene and the interruption it was causing. Unable to stand it any longer, he walked quickly out onto the floor, bent slightly forward, spent about two seconds looking for the lens, pointed at it, and held the point until the poor fellow with astigmatism crawled over to it and picked it up. A roar of appreciation went up from the Philadelphia crowd. Now they had seen Bradley do everything.

"The game itself was a nightmare," he remembers. "Shoot and miss. Shoot and miss." Penn State was leading 45-42 with about ten minutes to go. As it drew to an end, the game was both plodding and so close that it was clearly going to be a wretched way for either team to end its season—a misery which fell upon Penn State, 60-58.

The win was both interesting and significant, however, just because it was such an unkempt one. The pinnacle of a season for an Ivy League team had traditionally been a victory in the opening round of the N.C.A.A. tournament, and to win such a game, an Ivy team had always needed to be at the absolute top of its form. "But we figured that we had given about forty percent of our top," Bradley told me a couple of months later. "As a matter of fact, we didn't know what our top was. All of us felt the same way. If we could play that lackadaisically and lethargically and still beat a good team, then why couldn't we go somewhere?"

The eastern regional second round and finals were played in College Park, Maryland, in the University of Maryland's new indoor basketball stadium, which holds twelve thousand, five hundred people. The three winners from Philadelphia—Princeton, Providence, and St. Joseph's—would be joined there by

North Carolina State, which had beaten Duke to win
the championship of the Atlantic Coast Conference,
where basketball is usually so advanced an activity
that the Atlantic Coast Conference winner regularly
draws a bye past the opening round. As the draw
worked out, Princeton's first opponent in College
Park would be North Carolina State, which happened
to be celebrated for its zone press, a defensive tactic
designed to rattle the enemy into submission by har-
assing its players in all parts of the court.

The North Carolina State zone press had beaten
Duke's outstanding team, reason enough for Princeton to worry. Bradley and van Breda Kolff went into
New York to participate in a TV show two days before
the game. On the way home, they decided that the
Princeton team needed more confidence and experience against a zone press; so, after reaching the campus just before one a.m., Bradley spent more than an
hour going around to each player's room to tell him
to show up at the gym at ten a.m. for one last practice
before leaving for Maryland. Absorbed by hearing
about this pilgrimage in the dead of night, I asked
Bradley to tell me what they had all been doing. Five

had been asleep, four had been up studying or writing course papers, two had been up shooting the bull, and one had been discovered, even at that hour, with a ticket in his hand, in the act of scalping a townie.

Once the actual game with North Carolina State began, Bradley was surprised to notice that the North Carolina State players were playing without apparent emotion, and that they would pat Princeton players on the back after a Princeton score and say something like, "Nice play."

"That's no way to win," Bradley explained later. After the first ten minutes, he had felt that North Carolina State was finished. "Our defense was just eating them up," he remembered. "They couldn't move." North Carolina State's coach, Press Maravich, said later that his team was having even more trouble than that. "He's been written up in all the magazines," Maravich said. "He's the Number One basketball player in the country. He's the fourth best athlete in the world, according to the polls. Everybody reads that—you, me, my kids. So when he gets the ball, everybody stands around watching him. That's no way to play basketball. While we were watching him, he'd hit the open man behind us. It was as if we were hypnotized."

At one point, a North Carolina state player broke into the open with the ball and headed toward the basket for a lay-up. As he went up for the shot and was about to lay it in, a shadow came over him and Bradley, who had started a good twenty feet behind him, caught him and pinned the ball against the backboard. Gary Walters picked it up, as Bradley began to sprint toward the other end of the floor. Two or three seconds later, he took a high return pass from Walters, went up into the air with it, and scored. "In all my years," said the North Carolina State coach, "I have never seen that done."

The game was actually a fairly sloppy one in some respects, and van Breda Kolff was unimpressed. Bradley scored twenty-seven points but only hit four for eleven in the first half. "For a while there," said van Breda Kolff, "he was getting to be like everybody else. He was *trying* to make his shots." In the second half, Bradley hit six of seven. The final score was Princeton 68, North Carolina State 48. Princeton people were whooping and crowing because their team had gone so unbelievably far, and had won so easily, but van Breda Kolff, the professional basketball player in him coming right out with the truth, said, "It was a preliminary game, and it looked like one."

In the game immediately following the Princeton-North Carolina State game, Providence defeated St. Joseph's, 81-73. The Providence team had lost one game since their undefeated days when they had found Princeton's performance against Brown so amusing, but they were still the least defeated team in the United States; they were noted for their extraordinary speed, for the quickness of their hands, and for their deftness as athletes in a sport in which sheer height and muscle were often equipment enough. They were ranked in the national wire service polls as the fourth best team in the country, behind Michigan, U.C.L.A., and the team they had just beaten, St. Joseph's. It is no wonder, then, that the Providence players felt that with their victory over St. Joseph's they had virtually established themselves as the Eastern Regional Champions. They lifted one of their stars, Dexter Westbrook, onto their shoulders and he cut down the net.

This assumptive gesture helped get Princeton

ready for their own game with Providence the follow-
lowing night, and Westbrook contributed something
more when he told a reporter that in his view
Bradley was overrated. All during the day of the
game, the Princeton players kept encountering irritating remarks of similar nature, some from people
who had come to cheer them. The Ivy League is frequently accused of several kinds of snobbery, but
never in athletics. Ivy League people, in fact, have a
considerable sense of inferiority about the quality of
their teams in contrast to those of schools in other
parts of the country, and it is difficult even for rabid
alumni to imagine a Princeton team seriously competing with the best in the nation. A Princeton
alumnus went up to Bradley that afternoon and said,
"We're really proud of you. Do you think you have
a chance tonight?"

Bradley didn't actually read the newspapers that
day, but his eye happened to fall on a lead in the
Washington *Star* which said, in effect, that Princeton
would need five Bradleys and a good night to beat
Providence. "That triggered something," he remembers. He called a meeting and said to his teammates,

"We actually don't know how good we are. We have beaten the winner of the Atlantic Coast Conference with a good defense. We scored a hundred and seven points against Cornell with a good offense. We have never fully combined the defense and the offense."

Midway in the first half, the score was Providence 15, Princeton 15. Princeton's points had been scored almost evenly by four players, and the one who had yet to score dropped a twenty-foot set shot a minute later. Providence, playing smoothly itself, found that it was in a game with a basketball team as well as with a star. "I had been the dominant factor, at times, in other games," Bradley said, looking back, "but in the Providence game I was a member of the greatest team I had ever played on." They flew up the court in fast, interwoven patterns, and whipped the ball to one another so quickly that the people in the crowd didn't know where it was. They were all passing like Bradley. They were all shooting like Bradley, dribbling like Bradley, thinking like Bradley. Bradley hit a jump shot from the corner. Haarlow hit a jump shot from the corner. Rodenbach hit one from the top of the key. Bradley hit another one from the corner.

Brown—six feet nine—took a pass about fifteen feet out and scored on a driving lay-up. Walters sank a set shot from far out in the backcourt.

With eight minutes to go in the half, the score was Princeton 27, Providence 24. Princeton's defense was working well, and Providence was having trouble getting the ball in near the basket, but Providence played calmly, waiting for the pressure to drop. Haarlow hit one from the corner. Bradley hit an eight-foot jumper. Bradley hit a twenty-foot jumper. Hummer went two-for-two on the foul line. Walters hit a fifteen-footer. Rodenbach hit a fifteen-footer. Bradley hit a ten-footer. Haarlow went two-for-two on the foul line. Hummer scored on a drive. With eleven seconds to go, Bradley, on his way to the locker room, stopped, turned, and hit a twenty-five foot jump shot. The half-time score was Princeton 47, Providence 34.

There wasn't a lot that van Breda Kolff could say during the half. In the end, he said simply, "You're a better team than Providence. We can win this game."

The Providence coach, Joe Mullaney, was at the

same time deciding to handle Princeton by putting two men on Bradley, since Bradley had made most of the shots he had taken during the first half. After play had begun again, and this defense appeared, it was almost an indication that the game was over. Bradley went up into the air with the two men assigned to him, and, holding the ball above their hands, sent it into the basket. When Princeton got the ball again, Princeton's center, Robbie Brown, set a pick, and brought both of Bradley's defenders to a halt while Bradley moved past him toward the left side and hit a short fade-away jumper. The rest of the Princeton team began to score again, and they hit fifteen shots in a row. "It was the happiest I had ever been in my life," Bradley said, remembering that sequence. The final score was Princeton 109, Providence 69.

Bradley cut down the net and accepted the trophy for Princeton as winners of the eastern tournament. His unranked team had established itself as one of the four best in the country. He himself had made forty-one points, on thirteen of thirteen shots from the free throw line, and fourteen of twenty, or seventy-percent from the floor. The Princeton team's average was sixty-three percent. Naturally enough, the sports writers there unanimously named Bradley the tournament's most valuable player, and when the writers filled in their choices for the five-man all-tournament team, one of them wrote, "Bradley, Bradley, Bradley, Bradley, and Bradley." In the Princeton locker room, Dexter Westbrook, of Providence, worked his way through a lot of shouting people until he got to Bradley, shook his hand, and said, "It was a great game. You showed me something."

5. National Championships

The four teams which finally met in the Memorial Coliseum at Portland, Oregon, were Princeton, U.C.L.A., Wichita State University, and Michigan. Two and a half months after their first meeting in Madison Square Garden in December, Princeton and Michigan would play again. Both teams were more than pleased at the chance. Michigan's players were unsatisfied with the way their first victory had come about; and they were weary of hearing how Bradley had defeated them even though they had won the game. Princeton, for its part, obviously wanted to achieve the victory it had not quite held before. Bradley had told his depressed teammates in the locker room in Madison Square Garden in December that

129

there was one way to get at Michigan again—by winning the Ivy League, then winning the eastern championship. "And," he had said in a speech after the Providence game, "we did it."

This time, it was Michigan's night, and the score was decisive—93-76. Princeton led through much of the first half, but when Michigan took control it was fairly clear that Princeton was not going to lead again. At the half, Michigan was four points ahead, and when Bradley fouled out, as he had in December, Princeton was behind by six points, with six minutes to go. Bradley scored twenty-nine points, which was the high for both teams, and, reasonably enough, no one seemed to make much of the fact that Cazzie Russell scored twenty-eight. A game between Princeton and Michigan was by that time acknowledged to be a game between two basketball teams and not a match between two players, and the relative stature of Bradley and Russell, starting with the denominator that they were both All-Americans, had long since been established.

Paralleling Princeton's great disappointment, Michigan felt some of its own. In fact, the whole weekend in Portland was anything but what Michigan had hoped for, because they wanted an uncomplicated, undebatably clear-cut victory over Princeton, with Bradley in the game and functioning at his best all the way; and they then wanted to beat the western champion and prove that the polls had been correct all season in ranking Michigan number one. In the final game, however, U.C.L.A. beat Michigan for the national championship, 91-80. Meanwhile, Bradley had not been able to finish the Princeton-Michigan game, and—with something of an echo of the game which Princeton had played against Pennsylvania in Philadelphia in January—the officiating had been inconsistent enough to take a measure of the satisfaction of victory away from the winner.

Van Breda Kolff, who probably expends more ergs bellowing at referees than any other coach, nonetheless has an unusual sympathy for the job they have to do and the difficulties they encounter while doing it, particularly when they have to work a game with a star in it with a reputation such as Bradley's. "It was very difficult, and over the years the refs went both ways," van Breda Kolff remembers. "Sometimes they called them too close on him and sometimes, just because he was Bradley, they let him get away with murder." In the Princeton-Michigan game at Portland, Princeton drew so many fouls in the first half that they had to form a zone defense, as in Philadelphia, in order to keep Bradley and others in the game. The zone worked in two respects. It fairly well froze the margin between the scores of the two teams while Bradley was still playing, and it kept Bradley there for fourteen minutes of the second half. But Princeton was forced to play a Damoclean game, and Michigan did not have the opportunity to beat Princeton at its best because basketball is the only sport in which players can be permanently sent out of a game for fouls committed in the reasonable course of play. Michigan's players felt—correctly, I think—that they had a stronger team. They at least proved it in one way. They got fifty-six rebounds to Princeton's thirty-four, and it is almost axiomatic that a team which gets that many more rebounds than another will win. "I really feel that I failed in the Michigan game," Bradley said. "I failed as captain of the team. We weren't ready for that game mentally. The real place I failed was at half time. I should have had something to say. I sat there. I said something, but it wasn't much."

Having won a great victory over Providence and having lost to Michigan, there was nothing that Princeton could do in its final game that would either supersede the one or salvage anything from the other. Hence van Breda Kolff—who had been voted Coach of the Year only hours before the Michigan game— seemed to have a sizable problem in preparing his team for their playoff with Wichita, the midwestern regional champion. Princeton had a kind of responsibility in its final game not to move mechanically and dispiritedly around the court but to play as well as it could, to finish its season strongly, to prove to the remaining skeptic fringe that an Ivy League team was not out of place in a national final, and, in doing so, to make itself the third ranking team in the United States. All of that was true enough, but the Princeton players knew who belonged there and the effect of such exhortations was only enough to get them about halfway up for the game. In the end, the remark that set the fire came when van Breda Kolff said that no

team, after three years, should let a player like Bill
Bradley play his last game in anything but a win that
would not be forgotten.

The Princeton-Wichita game ended, as a contest,
when it had only been under way for about five
minutes and the score was Princeton 16, Wichita 4.
Princeton's team, as a unit, was shooting, dribbling,
passing, and rebounding at the top of its form.
Wichita tried to confuse Princeton and break its momentum by shifting rapidly back and forth from one
kind of defense to another, but Princeton, hitting
sixty-two percent from the floor, unconcernedly al-
tered its attack to fit the requirements of each defense. The score at halftime was Princeton 53,
Wichita 39, and later, with nine minutes and some
seconds to go, it was 84 to 58.

Princeton seemed to have proved what it needed to
prove, and Bradley, who by then had scored thirty-
two points, had been given the victory which van
Breda Kolff had said he deserved. The thirteen thousand people in the coliseum, who had reacted to the
previous games with a low hum and occasional polite
clapping, had been more typical of a basketball crowd,

apparently stirred by Princeton's ricochet passing and marvelously accurate shooting. Van Breda Kolff's team wasn't merely winning, it was winning with style.

But the game was over, and, one by one, van Breda Kolff began to take out his first team players, leaving Bradley in the game. Bradley hit a short one after taking the tap from a jump ball. He made two foul shots and a jumper from the top of the key. He put in two more foul shots, committed his own fourth personal foul, and looked toward van Breda Kolff in expectation of leaving the game; but van Breda Kolff ignored him. Getting the ball moments later, Bradley passed off to Don Roth. Smiling and shaking his head slightly, Roth returned the ball to Bradley.

There was a time-out and Bradley could hear people in the grandstands shouting at him that he ought to shoot when he got the ball. All of his team-mates crowded around him and urged him to let it fly and not worry about anyone else on the floor. Van Breda Kolff, calmly enough, pointed out to him that his career was going to end in less than five minutes and this was his last chance just to have a gunner's

go at the basket for the sheer fun of it. "So," remembers Bradley, "I figured that I might as well shoot."

In the next four minutes and forty-six seconds,
Bradley changed almost all of the important records
of national championship basketball. The most in-
tense concentration of basketball people to collect anywhere in any given year is of course at the national
championships, and as a group they stood not quite
believing, and smiling with pleasure at what they
were seeing. Bradley, having decided to do as everyone was urging him to do, went into the left hand
corner and sent up a long, high, hook shot. "I'm out
of my mind," he said to himself, but the shot dropped
through the net. "O.K.," he thought, moving back up
the court, "I'm going to shoot until I miss."

A moment later, sprinting up the floor through the
Wichita defense, he took a perfect pass, turned
slightly in the air and tossed the ball over his shoulder
and into the basket, with his left hand. The thirteen
thousand people in the crowd, Wichita's huge mission of fans included, reacted with an almost unbelievable roar to each shot as it went into the basket.
It was an individual performer's last and in some

ways greatest moment. Everyone in the coliseum knew it, and, to Bradley, the atmosphere was tangible. "There would be a loud roar," he remembered. "Then it was as if everyone were gathering their breath." Taking a pass at the baseline, he jumped above a defender, extended his arm so that the shot would clear the backboard, and sent a sixteen-foot jumper into the basket. Someone in the crowd started to chant, "I believe! I believe!," and others took it up, until, after each shot, within the overall clamor, the amusing chant could be heard.

From the left side, Bradley went up for a jump shot. A Wichita player was directly in front of him, in the air, too, ready to block it. Bradley had to change the position of the ball, and, all in a second, let it go. He was sure that it was not going to go in, but it did. Coming up the floor again, he stopped behind the key and hit another long jumper from there. Within the minute, he had the ball again and was driving up court with it, but a Wichita player stayed with him and forced him into the deep right-hand corner. Suddenly, he saw that he was about to go out of bounds, so he jumped in the air and—now really convinced that he was out of his mind—released a twenty-two foot hook shot, which seemed to him to be longer and more haphazard than any hook shot he had ever taken and certain to miss. It dropped through the net. Thirty seconds later, he drove into the middle, stopped, faked, and hit a short, clean jumper. Twenty seconds after that, he had the ball again and went high into the air on the right side of the court to execute, perfectly, the last shot of his career. With thirty-three seconds left in the game, van Breda Kolff took him out.

Princeton had beaten Wichita 118 to 82 and had scored more points than any other team in any other game in the history of the national championships, a record which had previously been set and re-set in opening rounds of play. Bradley had scored fifty-eight points, breaking Oscar Robertson's individual scoring record, which had been set in a regional consolation game. Hitting twenty-two shots from the floor, he had also broken Robertson's field goal record. His one hundred and seventy-seven points made against Penn State, North Carolina State, Providence, Michigan, and Wichita were the most ever made by any player

in the course of the national championships, breaking
by seventeen points the record held by Jerry West, of
West Virginia, and Hal Lear, of Temple. His sixty-
five field goals in five games set a record, too. His
team had also scored more points across the tournament than any other team ever had, breaking a record
set six years earlier by West Virginia. It had made
forty-eight field goals against Wichita, breaking a
record set by U.C.L.A.; and it had made one hundred
and seventy-three field goals in the tournament,
twenty-one more than Loyola of Illinois made in 1963
while setting the previous record and winning the
national championship. Where the names of three
individuals and four universities once appeared in the
records of the championships, only the names of
Bradley and Princeton now appear, repeated and repeated again.

The team record for most field goals in five games
was so overwhelming that it had already been set—at
a lower level—before Bradley began his final sequence
of scoring. But the other seven records had all been
set during his remarkable display, and to establish
them he had scored twenty-six points in nine minutes,

missing once. After van Breda Kolff and the others had persuaded him to forget his usual standards and to shoot every time he got the ball, he had scored— in less than five minutes—sixteen points without missing a shot.

6. *Points and Honors*

When Bradley returned to Princeton, he stood on top of the bus which had brought the team from the airport and began to apologize to a crowd of undergraduates for letting them down. "We didn't produce," he said. "I don't know whether to say I'm sorry . . ."

"Say it fifty-eight times," someone shouted, and Bradley's apologies were destroyed by applause.

He had been voted the most valuable player in the national championships. His fifty-eight points, made in his last game, had been his career high—and, through the whole game, he had made three of every four shots he had taken. His .886 final free-throw average for the season was the highest in the United

States. His season scoring average was over thirty points a game, and he had finished his career with two thousand, five hundred and three points, becoming, after Oscar Robertson, of Cincinnati, and Frank Selvy, of Furman, the third highest scorer in the history of college basketball.*

Conquerors of this sort usually follow up their homecomings with a lingering parade through the streets of Rome, but Bradley disappeared less than twenty-four hours after his return, having arranged to live alone in a house whose owners were away. Far enough from the campus to be cut off from it almost completely, he stayed there for a month—while a couple of hundred reporters, photographers, ministers, missionaries, Elks, Lions, Rotarians, TV producers, mayors, ad men, and fashion editors tried unsuccessfully to find him. His roommates, who fought off the

* This excludes Dickie Hemric of Wake Forest who, in four years rather than three, managed to compile more points than either Selvy or Bradley. Actually, with an entire extra season, Hemric only scored eighty-four points more than Bradley and forty-nine more than Selvy. It is interesting to note that Robertson, whose record is twenty-nine hundred and seventy-three points, is well over four hundred points above Selvy and Bradley, his nearest competitors. To fill out the theoretically unbeatable team that Bradley joined, the next three names below him on the list (four-year players omitted) are, in descending order, Elgin Baylor, Billy McGill, and Jerry West.

locusts that actually came to the campus, began to feel a little jaundiced about the invasions of society. Bradley, meanwhile, had gone into seclusion in order to write his senior thesis, and, working about fifteen hours a day for thirty days, he completed it. The thesis was thirty-three thousand words long, and he finished it one month to the day after the game with Wichita. It received a straight 1—grades at Princeton begin with 1 and end with 7—and Bradley was graduated with honors.

Meanwhile, a group of people in Princeton started the procedures necessary to change the name of their street to Bradley Court. The New York Knickerbockers, in order to protect themselves against any possibility that Bradley might change his mind about professional basketball and eventually play for another N.B.A. team, made him their first choice selection in the annual player draft. He heard from Oxford that, after his arrival there, he would be *in statu pupillari* at Worcester College.

And finally, his classmates at Princeton, not long before their graduation, summed him up in their "1965 Senior Class Poll," a rambling, partly serious and partly comical list of superlatives, ranging through eighty-one categories including "Biggest Socialite," "Biggest Swindler," "Most Brilliant," "Most Impeccably Dressed," "Most Ambitious," "Roughest," "Smoothest," "Laziest," "Hairiest," and "Most Likely to Retire at Thirty." Bradley was elected to none of these distinctions. He was named as "Most Popular" and "Most Likely to Succeed." As "Princeton's Greatest Asset," the Class of 1965 selected Bradley and a deceased woman who had just left the university twenty-seven million dollars. One category read: "Biggest Grind: Niemann, Lampkin; Thinks He Is: Bradley." His classmates also designated Bradley as the person they most respected. And, as a kind of afterthought, they named him best athlete.

Photographs

At Princeton, he was usually a little taller than the next man—the example here being Coleman Hicks, one of his roommates—but his appearance was otherwise indistinguishable from the enduring undergraduate mode: reading from the top down, he appeared to be part boy, part soldier, part construction worker. *Princeton University*

As a basketball player, he was so unbelievably accurate that he probably could have hit ten out of thirteen jump shots with this coconut. The fellow with the drums is another roommate, John Garber.

He was more interesting warming up than most players have ever been in play. In his last season, a kind of murmured chant would become audible in the grandstands as people counted aloud his shots dropping in.

When the action started, he could go like a five-foot ten-inch sprinter, and with all the coordination of a smaller man as well.

This is the passer. He is about ten feet from the basket. With the defense clearly beaten, he has the shot, and from that distance his chances of missing are about one

Richard M. Cion

in sixty. But he passes off to Don Rodenbach, who is a
little more in the clear, and one step away from an even
closer shot.

The over-the-shoulder shot had no actual name. He tossed it, without looking, over his head and into the basket. There was no need to look, he explained, because "you develop a sense of where you are."

Off the court, he would talk quite convincingly about his physical deficiencies, such as lack of speed and lack of spring. At least five other players on the court with him at this moment apparently lacked more than he did.

In the Olympic trials, held in the spring of 1964, he says that he was judged among the worst of the candidates in his ability to get high off the floor. His hips, here, are about seven feet up. He won his gold medal in Tokyo.

Starting from this crouch, his free throw never varied in its perfect form and consistent delivery. As a freshman, he made fifty-seven straight, an all-time record for the sport. As a senior, he was fouled so much that he scored two hundred and seventy-three points on free throws alone, making eighty-nine percent of them, the highest average in the United States.

Richard M. Cion

Four-on-one. (He hit the shot.)

Thos. H. Miner

Bradley analyzed his shots down to the last twitch of the last muscle. His hook shot came in five parts, of which this is the fifth.

Thos. H. Miner

The hook is the most difficult shot in the game. His was ambidextrous.

Richard M. Cion

Basketball, among other things, is a game of subtle felonies. Here he is positioning for a rebound. Notice his left hand.

Here, both his right hand and his left hand are finding
the mark.

Ordinarily, when he sat down, Princeton was far ahead. Both Bradley and Coach van Breda Kolff showed it.

On a couple of occasions, he fouled out toward the end of games that Princeton lost.

Jim Vincent

The Ivy League Championship was settled fairly early.

Richard M. Cion

This is the Ivy net. He cut another one two weeks later, when Princeton won the championship of the east.

Richard M. Cion

This seventeen-foot right-handed hook dropped into the net. It was, as basketball players often say in practice, "one to quit on"—it was Bradley's last shot in his last game at Princeton, but there was little sentiment about it. The last Pennsylvania game was, in effect, only a scrimmage before the national tournament.

R. P. Matthews

Merely by being in the eastern finals, Princeton had gone further in the national tournament than any Ivy League team in modern basketball history. Providence had lost only one game all season and no sportswriter thought there would be any contest at all. The assumption was misguided but correct. Princeton 109, Providence 69.

56

Princeton had made it as a team, and as a team they clobbered Providence. Bradley, for his part, hit seventy percent of his shots.

He scored forty-one points.

When the bus returned to Princeton, the undergraduates
massed to praise Allah.

Richard M. Cion

Each player spoke from the top of the bus. Here Bradley
listens to Don Roth, the team's No. 8 man and No. 1 wit.

Richard M. Cion

Bradley is a born speaker. People happening onto the scene and ignorant of its actual nature might have thought they were watching a nominee accepting the will of the convention.

In his last game, Bradley set four records for national championship play; his team set four others. He scored fifty-eight points.

Jim Vincent

John McPhee

This was taken at the end of the spring, after Bradley's comprehensive examinations and before his graduation from Princeton. It had been a crowded and exhausting year, but it didn't seem to have affected him at all.

1978 Addenda

After completing his work at Oxford, Bradley joined the New York Knickerbockers of the National Basketball Association. The contract negotiations that preceded this turn of events were arduous and complex. At one point, the president of the Madison Square Garden Corporation came out of the room saying, "That boy in there has a lawyer with him and he doesn't need him."

He played for New York for ten years, in the course of which he was married and made his home in New Jersey. In the off-season, he worked for—among others—the Office of Economic Opportunity, in Washington, and the Urban League street academies, in Harlem—and he wrote *Life on the Run,* an autobiographical narrative of the experience of a professional athlete. Through the winter he was, as Christopher Lehmann-Haupt once described him, the "gyroscope" of the Knicks—the thinker, the passer, the one who kept the offense five. The goal of his basketball life had been to be a starting player on a championship team. He missed it in high school and college. He reached it in 1970, again in 1973. With the exception of the domineering Boston Celtics, no other N.B.A. team in more than two decades has won the championship twice.

He retired in 1977, draping an arm around Red Holz-
man, his coach, who retired with him.

Instantly, he dove into a schedule of fourteen-hour days in his attempt to build a bridge from basketball to politics. A year later, he had strung enough cables to support a great deal of traffic at many levels, and he won over-whelmingly the nomination of the Democratic Party for United States Senator from New Jersey.

His home is in Denville, not far from Montclair State College, where his wife, Ernestine, is a professor of German and comparative literature. Their daughter, Theresa Anne, was born December 7, 1976.

1999 Addenda

Elected to the Senate three times, he concentrated his efforts on race relations, tax reform, water resources, children's health, global politics, and international trade. He gave up his seat after eighteen years in order to place himself in what he regarded as a more favorable position from which to seek a loftier job.

Ian Washington

While some people thought he was going into retirement, the only thing about him that was hung up to dry was his number 24, which he had worn as a starter on the Knickerbockers' only championship teams in the history of the New York franchise. At the shirt-retiring ceremony, he is seen here with Dave DeBusschere, his Knickerbocker roommate-on-the-road, whose number, 22, hangs high in Madison Square Garden near Bradley's.

Betty W. Sapoch

I met Bill Bradley when he was twenty and I was thirty-two. Over the years since then, he has laughed unrestrainedly at each and every political analysis I have ventured in his presence, has ignored essentially all commentary I have offered him on any number of his authorial manuscripts, performed the minor miracle of inspiring my wife to sit and watch basketball games at courtside, performed the minor miracle of inspiring *his* wife to sit and watch basketball games at courtside, entered one of my canoes and caused it to stand up on end on its way to capsizing, ruined my Volkswagen by driving it without oil, given me my vibrant goddaughter, and lost to me in a twenty-five-yard freestyle swimming race, after which he walked dripping to a telephone and withdrew from a pro-athletes' sport-a-thon he had agreed to take part in, in Florida. Our relationship, which began as a professional interview, is now as deep as its years, and is, well, brotherly. After *A Sense of Where You Are*, I did not write about him again—with a single exception. One of his signature habits as a New Jersey U.S. Senator was to walk the boardwalks and beaches in summer, talking to the people he encountered. Early on an August morning, he picked me up in Princeton and I went to the beaches with him. He was still there when the sun went down. I wrote a short piece about that day, titled "Open Man." The words that follow, among these pictures, are excerpted from that piece:

Betty W. Sapoch

Nine P.M. on the boardwalk at Seaside Heights, New Jersey, August 30, 1983. Against the black sky, lights revolve on wheels and whirling rides. Half a block west, off the edge of the glow, New Jersey's senior United States Senator is coaching two college-

age sisters, each of whom holds a placard saying "MEET SENATOR BRADLEY."

"You go out in front about twenty yards, stay apart, and funnel them in," he says, and the three step into the light.

Melchior DiGiacomo

"Hey, Bill!"

"Hey, big Bill!"

"Keep it up, Senator. You're doing a good job."

The device is as effective as it is simple. The girls are creating a V in the human river, and it is working like an eel trap.

"Man, are you tall! You looked small when you played for the Knicks."

"I *was* small when I played for the Knicks."

He weighs two hundred and five pounds, up zero from his weight in college. Which is not to imply a continuum. A year ago, his jowls were competing with the gross national product.

"Good job, Bill."

"Good to see you around, Senator."

"You've lost weight."

"I've lost about thirty pounds."

Senator Bradley has an athlete's contempt for exercise. He runs for office. To get rid of the thirty pounds, he developed the habit of eating lightly. He will work a twelve-hour day on half a sandwich and a cup of soup. Leaning forward as he walks—characteristically creating the impression that he is about to charge—he makes his way, shaking hands, from Shorty's Shish Kebab to Meat Ball City and on into the purview of the Arcade Skeeball. His haircut is fresh—a dark, rising wave in front, relief-mapping a bold headland flanked by a large bay. He wears a blue-and-white striped shirt with a button-down collar. His tie is brown and has small gold New Jerseys all over it like sea horses. His equine midriff is no bigger than it was when he played for the Knicks.

"Nice to meet you, Senator."

"Thank you. Where are you from?"

"Westfield. I go to Westfield High School. I had to write an essay about a fascinating American person, and I wrote about you."

"Did you get an A?"

"B-plus."

Generally speaking, middle-aged people in the crowd address him as Bill. Younger people call him Senator. Still younger people call him Bill. Nearly everyone is from New Jersey. Two out of three mention basketball.

A woman shakes his hand, turns to her several children, and says, "This is the next President. Remember what I said."

The next President reaches for another hand, in front of Sand Tropez. "Hello. Anything on your mind tonight?"

"Get teachers more money."

"Hello. How are you? Anything on your mind tonight?"

"What's going to happen in the Philippines?"

"There may be some changes; I don't know. I've long thought that we should move our bases to the Marianas, and not be beholden to a dictator."

"Senator Bradley! What a surprise! I just got a letter from you."

"Bill, Tom Berry. You may remember the name."

"Senator, my father met you the other night in the rest room at the Holiday Inn."

"Give me your autograph, please, like a good fella, Bill."

"Hey, I'm glad to meet you, Senator, but you gotta do something about the Philadelphia wage tax."

"Senator, the new auto-insurance rates are killing me. I've never had an accident."

"Senator, how do you feel about skateboards? Do you think skateboards should be allowed on the boardwalk?"

The question has arisen from a gentleman in short shorts who has recently become eligible to vote. Bradley is attentive to his arguments, which begin with the fact that he has invested forty dollars in the skateboard he holds in his hands. In this long day—in which the Senator has covered nearly three hundred miles—officials, editors, and miscellaneous citizens have sought his views on toxic waste, the telephone company, public transportation in southern New Jersey, Medicare, Social Security, internal revenue, nuclear safety, a nuclear freeze, the MX missile, violence in Sri Lanka, New York sewage, the Strategic Petroleum Reserve, the qualifications of schoolteachers, federal aid to education, bilingual education, the Reagan way with women and blacks, the Middle East, Central America, health care for senior citizens, the deregulation of natural gas, food waste, and the fingerprinting of bus drivers, and now, at nine-thirty in the evening, this shirtless citizen before him has raised the only issue for which he has not been prepared: skateboards on the boardwalk. He does not evade the question. Placing a hand on the kid's shoulder, he says, "Sure."

Melchior DiGiacomo

Ian Washington

•

The Senator got up at seven in Morris County, where he long ago hung his carpetbag, having been born and raised in Missouri, educated at Princeton and Oxford, and employed ten years in New York. The carpetbag is not a mere figure of speech. It is a handsome and capacious carpetbag, full of New Jersey mementos, and it hangs by the front door.

•

Senior senators tend to have license plates that say "U.S. SENATE 1." Bradley's plates say "881 KUW." The car is an old Olds, with two rock-impact craters in its windshield. The car appears to have been mugged. Bradley's Knickerbocker teammates used to say that Bradley was the person in New York least likely to be mugged, because his manner of rumply dress suggested that he had been mugged just moments before. There is no telephone in the car. To make his phone calls, he stops at diners, where he leans over pay telephones that come up to his hips.

•

"Would you accept the nomination for Vice-President?"

"No."

"As time goes by, is basketball mentioned less? Is it going away?"

"In part, yes. In part, no. I had a great ten years in basketball. It was rewarding in various ways—and has been, frankly, in this job."

"When you were playing basketball, did you take muscle-building drugs?"

"Obviously not," muttered the low voice of a fly on the wall.

•

Through time, Bradley has acquired some touches of the accents of New Jersey, where new cars are filled with un-let-it and one hears the shortest "a"s known to diction.

•

And now, on the boardwalk in Seaside, 10 P.M., he says goodbye to the citizen with the skateboard and moves along through another half mile of crowd.

"Hey, Bill!"

"There's Dollar Bill!"

Whether for a town meeting or a college conference on a specific subject or a walking town meeting

("You go where the people are"), he will be up at seven in the morning to do this sort of thing all day tomorrow, and the next day and the next, and a day or two a week in New Jersey while the Senate is in session. On sheer fatigue and vegetable soup, he sways a little and his eyes are glazed.

In front of the Seaside Coin Castle, he is asked to explain American participation in the International Monetary Fund. He is asked to shoot a basket (declined). He is asked "to keep the Commies on the other side of the ocean."

"Hey, big Bill."

"You gotta do something about the Knicks, Bill."

A two-year-old child coming toward him in a stroller is wearing camouflage-cloth battle dress from hat to foot and is carrying a plastic automatic weapon. The man pushing him runs forward, takes Bradley's elbow, and pulls him toward the child, saying, "Senator, you've got to shake hands with this man." The Senator lifts a tiny hand from the rifle, gives a squeeze, and moves on.

"Nice to meet you, Bill."

"Nice to meet you, Senator."

"What job bills before Congress do you support?"

"You were a big help to my daughter in getting her boyfriend over from Scotland."

"Senator Bradley, you helped me get Social Security for the disabled."

"Keep it up, Senator."

"Stay in there, Bill."

"Are you the best foul shooter in the Senate?"

"I'm the *only* foul shooter in the Senate."

Emma Byrne